THE OPEN UNIVERSITY

**An Arts Foundation Course
Units 13, 14 and 15**

Introduction to Philosophy

Prepared by Rosalind Hursthouse for the Course Team

The Open University Press

The Open University Press
Walton Hall, Milton Keynes
MK7 6AA

First published 1978

Designed by the Media Development Group of the Open University.

Printed in Great Britain by
EYRE AND SPOTTISWOODE LIMITED
AT GROSVENOR PRESS PORTSMOUTH

ISBN 0 335 05415 3

This text forms part of an Open University course. The complete list of units in the course appears at the end of this text.

For general availability of supporting material referred to in this text, please write to Open University Educational Enterprises Limited, 12 Cofferidge Close, Stony Stratford, Milton Keynes, MK11 1BY, Great Britain.

Further information on Open University courses may be obtained from the Admissions Office, The Open University, P.O. Box 48, Walton Hall, Milton Keynes, MK7 6AB.

1.1

CONTENTS INTRODUCTION TO PHILOSOPHY

UNIT 13 SUBJECTIVITY AND SCEPTICISM
CONTENTS

IMPORTANT NOTE

In these units you will notice that, in addition to the familiar double lines,

I have also used a large dot •. I have done this to emphasize how important it is that you should work out your own answers to questions – and write them down, in your notebook – before seeing what I myself go on to say. So: whenever you see the dot, *stop* and try to answer the question before reading on.

For Unit 14, you will also need to use the Masking Card which is bound in at the end of the book: tear it out now. Instructions for its use are on page 49. On the card are various definitions referred to in Unit 14. They have been reprinted at the end of the unit (page 79), in case your card goes astray.

In the course of Units 13–15 you will be asked to look at the *Supplementary Texts* and also to re-read certain passages in Units 3–5, so keep these by you as you work.

INTRODUCTION

The failure of philosophers to produce a crisp, adequate definition of their own subject has become a standing joke. Most introductory books on philosophy have a long preamble, explaining why it is so hard to say what philosophy is, and devoting much space to saying what it isn't.

Figure 1   The philosopher getting in a tangle trying to define his own subject

In the old Arts Foundation Course, A100,[1] Godfrey Vesey introduced the philosophy units by saying:' . . . it might be said that the way to find out what philosophy is, is to do philosophy, to philosophize. Where shall we start?' This seems to me by far the best way. We are going to start with a unit on scepticism (a *sceptic* is someone who denies that we know anything, or many things, for certain), to be followed by one on value judgements and ethics, and a third on 'epistemology'. 'Epistemology' means 'the theory of knowledge', from the Greek word *episteme* meaning 'knowledge'. In each of the three units I introduce you to a very standard philosophical problem and I chose to do this for several reasons.

One reason is that you have to start philosophizing by jumping straight into the deep end, because it is not a subject which, as it were, has a shallow end. In a Tom Stoppard play, there is a character who thinks he would like to become a philosopher and imagines starting off as a philosopher's apprentice. He is not quite sure what this would involve but thinks he would go into the office early, tidy the desk, sort out a few paradoxes and perhaps, as time goes on, get to being allowed to solve *one* horn of a dilemma.

It is a charming idea but not, alas, feasible. For suppose I began by giving you one horn of a dilemma to solve. How would you know that it *was* a horn of a dilemma? I should have to explain the whole dilemma. Once I had done that it would probably still not be clear how and why the problem had arisen in the first

[1] The Open University (1971) A100 *Humanities: A Foundation Course,* The Open University Press.

6

place. So I should have to explain how one philosopher had argued that such and such, but that this was wrong because so and so; and why another philosopher had then argued that this and so . . . And by then you would be up to your neck in arguments – straight in at the deep end.

So, given the nature of philosophy, I have to introduce you to it by starting you off on standard philosophical problems. There *are* no beginner's problems.

Perhaps for this reason most people do find philosophy difficult; many find it off-putting. I have tried to make it seem less awesome by writing, deliberately, in a very informal, conversational, style. I hope you don't find it irritating; if you do, all I can suggest is that you try to ignore it and concentrate on the philosophy. Whether you like the style or not, don't be misled by it. It is *not* casual; I have chosen my words with care. It was *not*, for me, the easy way out. It was done in the hope that it would help you to understand and enjoy philosophy. It is not mere chat. Philosophy is a subject which makes great demands of concentration. Many of the students we tried these units out on found it necessary to backtrack and re-read fairly frequently, though they had not needed to in earlier units. But there is no extra reading material associated with the first two philosophy units and only a little with the third, so even the students who backtracked a lot still did not fall behind in their work.

If you find yourself with time in hand and are finding the philosophy easy, then of course you should read the material in the *Supplementary Texts*, but I do emphasize that it is optional.

My main reason for selecting these three topics – scepticism, value judgements and epistemology – was that they gave me a theme. They sound like three quite separate topics, but they are linked by a continuing concern with the many ways of viewing a distinction which is of central importance in the study of the arts, namely, the distinction between the *subjective* and the *objective*.

Ossie Hanfling said, near the beginning of Units 2B and 9 (page 8), 'Well then, isn't argument perhaps less appropriate in the arts than in such fields as science and mathematics? (Aren't those people – scientists and mathematicians – always trying to *prove* something?) Let us agree that there is also a place for argument in such arts subjects as history and philosophy. But what about – arts? Isn't art a matter of feeling rather than logic? Listening to Beethoven, who cares about reasons and arguments?'

Perhaps you didn't react that way, or perhaps not quite so strongly. But although we mightn't go so far as to say *who cares* about reasons or arguments in the arts subjects, it is natural to worry about what the reasons or arguments are meant to be like. It *is* natural to group science and mathematics together, saying they are concerned with objective proof and truth, and to contrast them with the arts subjects, where objective proof seems impossible and truth a matter of subjective opinion.

This is worrying if you have decided to *study* the arts. If the arts units do *not* contain objective truths, why do we read them? If objective proof is impossible, how can we prove that the author of the unit is wrong if we disagree with what he says? (As I heard someone say plaintively at summer school, 'Why does my tutor give me a tick in the margin when I say what the unit author thinks but write "Subjective!" when I say what *I* think?')

If you have started worrying about subjectivity, you have started worrying about a philosophical problem; in fact, a whole set of problems. They do not have a simple answer and we do not have time to go into any of them very deeply. But I hope that these units will encourage you to think about them constructively and philosophically.

Obviously, I cannot do your thinking for you, nor can I teach you to think philosophically without your active co-operation. Learning philosophy is not a matter of learning a set of philosophic truths: it is a matter of learning to *do* philosophy, of acquiring a skill or technique. Acquiring a skill or technique requires practice. There will be occasions in the units where I ask you questions because I want you to try to think out answers for yourself, that is, to practise doing philosophy. Trying to think out answers for yourself is much *much* more important than hitting on the right answer by guesswork, or just passively taking in what I say. I'm not saying your own answers, whatever they may be, are of intrinsic value; I'm saying the effort to get to them is of intrinsic value. You will find that there are some questions you are obviously meant to get right – for instance, the ones labelled 'comprehension questions' – but others I just want you to *try*. Getting you to try, and then giving my own answer, is the nearest I can get on paper to the ideal way of teaching philosophy, which is in a face-to-face tutorial, with one tutor, one student, engaged in the co-operative activity of trying to get at the truth.

1 SUBJECTIVITY

1.1 ARTHUR MARWICK ON 'THE SUBJECTIVE ELEMENT IN HISTORY'

There are two subjective elements

You will notice that in the quotation from Ossie Hanfling's unit, it was suggested that perhaps history and philosophy are more like science and maths than the other arts subjects are. You may also remember that the respects in which history differed from, and was like, the sciences, was a topic that Arthur Marwick spent some time discussing in Unit 3. In this context he discussed 'the subjective element' in history. When he did *that*, he started doing philosophy, and I am going to take him up on it.

I said in the introduction that the topics of these units were linked by a continuing concern with the *many* ways of viewing the distinction between the *subjective* and the *objective*. Naturally I haven't defined these terms – if I gave a definition this would immediately limit us to just *one* way of viewing the distinction. 'Subjective', in particular, is a term that can be defined in many different ways and we shall be discussing some different possible definitions in the next unit. But a definition in a vacuum often gives one nothing but an illusion of understanding. The aim of this part of the unit is for us to get clear about what sort of subjective element is shared by history and the natural sciences, *not* by slapping down the definition of 'subjective' involved, but by a careful process of discussion and elimination.

I'm using Arthur Marwick's unit as a starting point because I think it important that you should link different parts of the course. So please will you go back to Unit 3 and re-read, very quickly, section 4 (pp. 30–32) and the first part of section 6 (pp. 44–46) just to remind yourself of what he said.

As you read, ask yourself the question, 'Does Marwick think history has *two, different* subjective elements, or just one?' for I am going to argue that he is committed, in these passages, to two subjective elements. There is one subjective element which history does *not* share with all the other disciplines (e.g. science), which we could call 'the moral element' to single it out. And there is a *second*, different, subjective element which, according to Marwick, history *does* share with all disciplines, including science. Make a note of any passages that are relevant to your answer. Please re-read Marwick now.●

DISCUSSION

Despite the fact that section 4 is called '*The* subjective element . . .', I think that Marwick is discussing two, different elements, both of which can be called 'subjective' because 'subjective' can be defined in so many different ways. He discusses one subjective element which history and science both have; and another, the moral element, which history has and science hasn't. So he is committed to two. That's what I think. The next question is – Why do I think that? What are my grounds?

In what follows I am making sure that whatever my grounds are, they could also be grounds *you* have. That is, I haven't slipped along to Arthur Marwick and got the answer 'straight from the horse's mouth'. For the purposes of this exercise I am putting myself in your position, and limiting myself to the text. So the question before us is 'What are *the* grounds, in the text, for saying that the unit author is committed to two, different, subjective elements in history?'

From page 45 I gather that the author thinks history contains one subjective element which science does *not* contain, namely that involved in making (moral) value judgements. He says, ' . . . there are times when the historian simply cannot avoid making value judgements of a type *not* encountered in the natural sciences', and later he says the same thing: ' . . . the historian sometimes must be involved in making value judgements: this *does* distinguish him from the scientist.' (My emphasis both times.)

Although the quotations mention merely value judgements, I'm assuming these are *moral* value judgements (a) because of his examples ('massacre', 'faction', etc.) and (b) because he refers us back to an exercise in section 4 (page 31). It is the example of bad boring history which *is* bad and boring precisely because the writer is refusing to make any *moral* judgements about the people and countries involved.

So, according to Marwick, moral judgements enter into history but not into the natural sciences, and in *that* sense history has a subjective element which science does not have. Let's call it 'the moral element' for the moment.

But from various other remarks in the text, I gather that Marwick thinks that in some *other* sense, science, indeed all disciplines, have a subjective element. Page 30: ' . . . to a degree this is true also of the sociologist, the geographer, and even of the natural scientist.' Page 32: 'History does contain a subjective element. But this is true of other subjects, even science subjects . . .' Page 45: ' . . . the scientist is never absolutely and completely objective.' Page 32: 'All disciplines do in fact have a slight subjective element in them', including perhaps even mathematics, since he continues: '(Some of you will be in a position to note that mathematics as taught in the Foundation Course in Mathematics at this university differs considerably from the mathematics you may have been taught elsewhere.)'

The exercises on pp. 31–32 certainly suggest that *this* subjective element is simply what I called the moral element. The moral element is what the example of bad boring history lacks, and we imagine that it is the inevitable *moral* element which is going to reveal that one scholar is a German and another a Roman Catholic and another a communist, etc. But the moral element *can't* be the subjective element which history shares with the other disciplines, e.g. science, because Marwick says that science *doesn't* have the moral element.

So, according to Marwick, there is some subjective element (not the moral element) which history and all disciplines, have. History also has the moral element. (See above.) So history has two, different, subjective elements.

1.2   WHAT IS THE SECOND ELEMENT?

What is this subjective element that history *shares* with science? Marwick says that 'the historian can never entirely escape from the influences of the age and environment in which he lives' (page 30). This fact (that the historian can never entirely escape, etc.) seems to be what introduces the second subjective element into history. So it should be true of the scientist as well, and introduce the second subjective element into science.

Let's think about this. In what way is it true that the *scientist* cannot entirely escape from the influences of the age and environment in which he lives? 'Well,' we might think, 'scientists are humans like the rest of us; it is humans or persons who do the experiments and observe the results.' As Marwick says, 'the setting up of a piece of scientific apparatus . . . must involve something of the human personal element' (page 32), and 'scientific observation . . . is still *human* observation' (page 45).

But is the fact that it is humans or persons who do the scientific experiments and observe the results sufficient to prove the existence of a *subjective* element in *Marwick*'s sense, that is, a sense in which science is 'biased', 'not strictly in accordance with the facts, but influenced by personal feelings and prejudice'? (His definition, page 30.)

I think not. Saying that it is humans or persons who do the experiments and observe the results does not automatically bring in bias, personal feelings and prejudice. No doubt scientists, as people, have their biases, feelings and prejudices; no doubt these are influenced by their age and environment – but do bias, feelings and prejudice enter into such things as setting up experiments and reading off figures? And if not, where is there room for the influence of age and environment on the *scientist*, when he is doing science?

Of course, bias, personal feelings and prejudice *can* enter in the form of experiment the scientist chooses to set up and the way in which he chooses to interpret his results. A notorious example of this would be some of the ⌐proofs¬[1] that American negroes are not as intelligent as whites. The negroes did indeed do less well on the IQ tests, but the results were open to at least two interpretations. You can take them as proving white intellectual superiority or, as people were quick to point out, you can take them as proving that IQ tests designed for educated middle-class children are a poor test of the IQ of semi-illiterate slum children. And certainly, at least *some* of the people who interpreted the results the first way were biased and prejudiced.

So far so good. *Some* science *can* have a subjective element. But we can't move from there to 'So all science must have a subjective element.' Isn't it only in certain areas, such as the social sciences, that this kind of prejudice can enter? Can it enter into physics, for example?

I don't think it can. But something else does, and I think Marwick puts his finger on it (unfortunately in the context of the moral element). He says, '*in the mere selection of his facts*, the historian is involved in judgement of a sort' (page 45, my italics). Now *that* sort of judgement does not have to be a moral judgement; it does not have to be influenced by personal feelings or prejudice, but it does have to be made. And the same is true even in physics.

1.3   THE FACTS DON'T SPEAK FOR THEMSELVES

In what way do scientists have to exercise judgement in selecting their facts? Well, *which* facts are to count as the decisive confirmation or disproof of a theory, *which* facts are to be hung on to *as* facts despite apparent counter-evidence; how typical or representative a fact is, and of what – these are things which the scientist and even the mathematician have to decide. They are not matters on which the facts speak for themselves.

These remarks do not make much sense without examples. Here is one. As recently as the 1920s, a chemist ran a set of experiments on an iron oxide compound, and, to his surprise, instead of confirming Dalton's Law of Definite Proportion,[2] the results of the experiments went against it. The chemist did the experiments again and again with the same results – and concluded that he must have made a mistake somewhere. As it turned out, his mistake lay in drawing

---

[1] These are called 'scare quotes'. You put them around a word or phrase when you don't quite intend to say what the word or phrase means. See Units 2B and 9, pp. 18–19 (though Oswald Hanfling does not use the special scare-quote symbol I use here).

[2] Dalton's Law says, roughly, that in simple compounds which consist of atoms of different elements, the ratios of the atoms are in simple proportions, e.g. water has *two* atoms of hydrogen to *one* of oxygen; common salt has *one* of sodium to *one* of chlorine. A compound that went against Dalton's Law would have, say, 29 atoms of one element to 16 atoms of another.

that conclusion. We now know that Dalton's Law does not apply to all cases; in particular not to metal alloys. But the facts did not force the chemist to conclude that Dalton's Law had exceptions. In so far as the facts ⌜spoke⌝, all they did was present him with an alternative. What they ⌜said⌝ was, 'Either the current theory is wrong *or* you have made a mistake setting up your experiment.' And the chemist decided to plump for the latter – mistakenly, as it turned out.

[ɪ]

PHILOSOPHIÆ
NATURALIS
Principia
MATHEMATICA

Definitiones.

Quantitas _____ *m orta ex illius Denſitate &*
_____ *junɛtim.*

A Er _____ patio quadruplus eſt.   Idem
in _____ us per compreſſionem vel lique-
factionem _____ ratio corporum omnium, quæ
per cauſa _____ e condenſantur.   Medii interea,
ſi quod fue _____ libere pervadentis, hic nullam ra-
tionem habe _____ antitatem ſub nomine corporis vel
Maſſæ in ſ _____ ligo. Innoteſcit ea per corporis cu-
_____ rtionalem eſſe reperi per expe-
_____ ſtituta , uti poſthac docebi-

Def.

Figure 2   Isaac Newton (1643–1727). Note that his treatise is called 'Mathematical Principles of Natural Philosophy'. Cf. Radio Programme 13

Here's another example. As you may know, Einsteinian theory has supplanted Newtonian in physics; what many people don't know is that the two theories coincide for ordinary sorts of distances, so that Newton's assumption that the laws of planetary motion govern matter right down to its ultimate constituents, only fails us in sub-atomic physics. Most of the facts we observe around us in this world don't ⌜say⌝: 'Newton is wrong and Einstein is right.' Newtonian theory enables us to build skyscrapers and bridges and hydroelectric schemes. But the trouble was, we took these facts as being typical or representative of the most general facts about space and energy and matter – and that turned out to be a mistake, as Einstein showed. But the facts never, as it were, ⌜*said*⌝: 'We are typical or representative.' Before Einstein, the scientists interpreted them that way. And now, some people say, it is turning out that Einsteinian theory is failing to apply to some phenomenon they call black holes.

So even in science (and maths., though the only examples I know are too complicated to include) the facts do not simply speak for themselves. They need interpretation, and the scientist, like the historian, has to exercise judgement in selecting them. *So* . . . now, how shall I express my conclusion? Should I say, '*So*, science has a subjective element'?

Well, I don't think I should do that, because if I do, I shall be taken to mean something that I don't mean and it will be thought that I agree with a lot of people I do not agree with. That brings us to the next section.

1.4 REVISION OF THE PRECEDING SECTIONS

Before we go on to the next section proper, I am going to give you a short summary of what has been said so far. Before reading mine you should try to write your own. If you find writing summaries fairly easy, go straight ahead and do it. If you find them difficult (a) turn to the table of contents and (b) answer the following questions in complete and informative sentences. (By that I mean something like this. The first question is 'What is the first thing discussed?' If you answer that in an *in*complete sentence, you write 'Unit 3'. If you answer it in a complete sentence you write 'The first thing discussed is Unit 3.' Though complete, that is about as uninformative as you can be while still answering the question. If you were being informative you would write, for example, 'The first thing discussed is Marwick on the subjective element in history' or 'The first thing discussed is Marwick on subjectivity in history' or even 'The unit begins with a critical analysis of Marwick's discussion of subjectivity.')

Here are the questions. If you answer them in the way I have suggested the summary should almost write itself. If you find this starting to happen, feel free to alter the order of the questions, or answer two in one sentence; I shall write my summary like that. (Remember to use the table of contents.)

1 What is the first thing discussed?

2 How many subjective elements is Marwick committed to (according to the text)?

3 What is the first?

4 Is it (according to the text) an element which history shares with science?

5 Is the second element one that history shares with science?

6 Is this second element easy to identify?

7   What does it come down to? (What point is made?)

8   Should we conclude, simply and straightforwardly from this point, 'So science has a subjective element'?●

MY SUMMARY

(1) The first thing discussed is Marwick on what he called '*the* subjective element in history'. Despite this 'the', (2) Marwick is committed not to one but to two subjective elements. (3) The first is what might be called the moral element. (4) According to the text, it is an element which history does *not* share with science and hence it must be different from another element which, (5) according to the text, *is* shared by science. (6) This second element proved hard to identify but eventually (7) it comes down to the point that in the mere selection and interpretation of his facts the scientist is involved in judgement of a sort. The facts do not speak for themselves, but need interpretation. But (8) we should not conclude simply and straightforwardly from this point, 'So science has a subjective element.'

Why shouldn't we? Because if we do, we shall be misunderstood. That is the reason, and the topic of the next section.

1.5   THE REASON WHY WE SHOULD NOT CONCLUDE, 'SO SCIENCE HAS A SUBJECTIVE ELEMENT'

If, before you had read this unit, you had seen an advertisement for a lecture or a radio programme called 'The subjective element in science', would you, honestly, have expected it to be about the point that the facts need interpretation? I wouldn't have. 'Science has a subjective element' sounds so much more striking than 'Scientists need to interpret the facts; the facts do not speak for themselves.' It has precisely that dramatic 'You won't believe this but . . .' ring about it that Ossie Hanfling warned us about in Units 2B and 9. Now what is this dramatic thing that we won't believe? What can it be but this: 'All those differences you used to think there were between poetry and science, or history and science – well, those differences don't exist. Scientists are human like the rest of us, and they can't keep their feelings, biases and prejudices, the influences of their age and environment, out of their science.'

This dramatic claim is the natural way to take 'Science has a subjective element.' We would naturally expect a radio talk entitled 'The subjective element in science' to be about how the feelings, biases and prejudices of scientists couldn't be kept out of their science. We would naturally take someone who said 'Science has a subjective element' to mean that scientists' judgements are inescapably biased, prejudiced, influenced by the age and environment in which they live, etc. I haven't said whether I think that is true or not; but it certainly does *not* follow from my saying that the scientist, like the historian, has to exercise judgement in the selection and interpretation of his facts.

There are some people who do think that science is subjective in the sense of the dramatic claim. Some people, for instance, think that it is blind, unreasoning, twentieth-century, anti-spiritual, Western prejudice that leads scientists to believe that Uri Geller is a fake.

Figure 3 Uri Geller. I am writing this unit in 1976. In years to come Geller may be quite forgotten. He hit the headlines in about 1973, claiming that he could bend forks and keys, and do similar things involving the movement of matter, by the power of thought. Newspapers reported that he had done these things before a collection of scientists who had searched him most carefully beforehand for hidden loops of wire or magnets. Other newspapers reported that on some test occasions his powers failed him. At least one professional magician claimed that he could duplicate Geller's results and also (very interestingly) that it would take a trained magician (rather than a scientist) to set up a proper control experiment, because only a trained magician would know what to look for and look out for

Such people say at least two things. First they can agree with us that the facts don't speak for themselves. Faced with Geller and his forks we can interpret the facts as 'Geller is a clever fake' *or* as 'Geller can alter the shape of metal forks by the power of thought.' And this is like the example of the chemist and his experiments.

Secondly, the Uri Geller supporters go on to give a special explanation of why scientists plump for the description 'Geller is a clever fake' rather than the description 'Geller can alter the shape of metal forks by the power of thought.' The explanation given is that the scientists dismiss the idea of the power of mind over matter out of pure prejudice. Either because they live in the twentieth century, rather than the middle ages, *or* because they live in Western society, rather than in a culture which accepts spiritual intervention as a matter of course, *or* because they are frightened to admit the unknown and mysterious into their science, *or* for some other similar reason, the scientists, so the Uri Geller supporters say, settle for the first description – 'Geller is a clever fake.' And they (the Uri Geller supporters) go on to say, 'So science has a subjective element.'

Now their grounds, as I have sketched them here, are not compelling. For one thing, they have to maintain that *every* scientist who has dismissed Geller as a clever fake has done so out of prejudice. But the belief that Geller is a fake, though it *may* turn out to be false, and may be believed by *some* scientists because they are prejudiced, can also be believed on good grounds and not simply because of prejudice. All the science we have, to say nothing of all past evidence of past fakes, gives us grounds for saying it is extremely unlikely that he is anything else. Relying on all the science we have, and not believing what is extremely unlikely, is not blind, unreasonable or prejudiced.

Despite the fact that their grounds are not compelling, the Uri Geller supporters do have the *right sort* of grounds for saying, 'Science has a subjective element.' They *do* have grounds which are to do with bias, prejudice, feelings, influence of age and environment. If they conclude, on *those* grounds, 'So science has a subjective element', they will naturally be taken to mean just what they *do* mean. *They* won't be misunderstood.

But if I conclude, on the grounds that the facts don't speak for themselves, 'So science has a subjective element', I will naturally be taken to mean the same as them, which I don't.

What a fool I would look if I became involved in a radio talk on the subjectivity of science.

Me: Science has a subjective element.

Interviewer: Really? Why do you say that? (= What are your grounds?)

Me: Well, the facts don't speak for themselves. The scientist has to interpret them.

Int: *(reasonably enough):* And you think he can't help giving them a biased interpretation, being swayed by his feelings and prejudices?

Me: No, no! I suppose that does happen occasionally but I'm sure it doesn't happen often. I don't mean anything like that.

Int: Oh. Well, you mean the scientist is inevitably influenced by his age and environment? For instance, he can only use existing concepts and hence is blinkered by the prejudices of his age and environment?

Me: No, no. Sometimes big strides in science come just because a scientist finds a new way of interpreting the facts and invents a new concept.

Int: *(getting confused):* Well, are you saying anything about the feelings, biases, prejudices, influences of age and environment at all?

Me: No.

Int:. *(understandably irritated):* Then why on earth did you say that science had a subjective element?

Me: *(sheepishly):* I don't know.

If I want to avoid being exposed like this, I think I should avoid saying that science has a subjective element, *given* that my only ground for that assertion is the point about the facts needing interpretation.

Of course if someone, for instance a Uri Geller supporter, has *different* grounds, grounds that *do* have something to do with bias, feelings, influence of age and environment, etc., then that person can go ahead and say, 'Science has a subjective element' without having my worry about being misunderstood. He will naturally be taken to mean that the scientists' judgements are inescapably biased, prejudiced, etc. and that will be just what he *does* mean.

But it is not what I mean, so if I say, 'Science has a subjective element' I shall be taken to mean something I don't mean. Which is a reason against concluding, 'So science has a subjective element' at the end of section 1.3.

1.6 A SENSE OF 'SUBJECTIVE' IN WHICH WE COULD CONCLUDE, 'SO SCIENCE HAS A SUBJECTIVE ELEMENT'

The argument in the preceding section could be caricatured as amounting to the following:

> 'Science has a subjective element' means 'Scientists' judgements are inescapably biased, prejudiced, etc.' So you shouldn't say, 'Science has a subjective element' unless what you mean is that scientists' judgements are inescapably biased, prejudiced, etc.

After looking at the title of *this* section, can you see an objection to this argument? Please write your answer down.●

DISCUSSION

As long as your answer says something like, ' "Science has a subjective element" can mean more than one thing, because "subjective" can mean more than one thing', that is all I was after. You might have been more thorough, but the idea of more than one meaning is enough.

Now I'll do a thorough objection to the actual (not the caricatured) argument in the preceding section. Someone might object like this: 'You claimed that if you said, "Science has a subjective element" you would be taken to mean that scientists' judgements were inescapably biased, prejudiced and all the rest of it. But you could avoid that. You said yourself (page 9) that the word "subjective" is vague and can be defined in lots of different ways. One thing "subjective" can be used to mean is, very generally, personal or human involvement of any sort. And it does follow from what you said about scientists having to interpret the facts that science does have a subjective element, *in the sense* that it has an uneliminable human or personal element (i.e., the interpretation). So why not say that?'

What do you think of this objection? Is it a sound (good) one or not? Please write your answer down.●

DISCUSSION

I think it is a good one. I needn't have made quite such a fool of myself in the imaginary radio talk – I could have started by saying, 'Science has a subjective element, BY WHICH I MEAN NO MORE THAN THAT it has an uneliminable human or personal element.' Then the interviewer wouldn't have misunderstood me so drastically.

Although the objection is sound, misunderstanding is not *quite* so easily avoided as it suggests. If I am on the radio with a whole lot of Uri Geller supporters, it will be hard both for the interviewer and the audience to remember that I am using the word 'subjective' in a different sense from the others. Further confusion will result from the phrase 'science has a human or personal element', because although all *I* mean by 'the human element' is 'the human interpretations and selections', in the context of the radio talk entitled 'The subjectivity of science' everyone will probably forget, and will take me to be talking about bias, personal feelings and prejudice. Even if we carefully specify what we mean by 'subjective' we shall still have to be on the watch for further mis-understandings.

Well, let's suppose not only that we have carefully specified that by 'subjective' we mean no more than personal or human involvement, but also that we are on our guard about further misunderstandings (about, for example, the nature of involvement – not feelings, only interpretations) – *then* can we conclude, 'So science has a subjective element'?

Yes, I think we can.

But now suppose someone says the following: 'Even if you carefully specify what you mean by "subjective", the word still doesn't lose all its shock value. "Science has a subjective element" goes on sounding startling, however much you qualify it.'

What do you think of that? Do you think it shows that, even with the qualifications we shouldn't say, 'Science has a subjective element'? Or do you want to respond, 'Well, so what? Why shouldn't it sound startling? The point that, even in science, interpretation of the facts is required *is* startling.' You needn't make up your mind on this one. Just think about it before reading on.●

I have been talking up to now as though the point that even in science interpre-tation of the facts is required were quite obvious and nothing startling. That was not very frank of me, since I think it is far from obvious, and, speaking per-sonally, when it was first pointed out to me, I was very startled indeed. If someone just said, 'Of course facts need to be interpreted' one might react with no more than 'Of course, of course. Naturally they need to be interpreted', and think no more about the matter. But if someone says, 'So science is *subjective*. The interpretation is *human* interpretation', it gives one quite a jolt. Therein lies the usefulness of the shock value of 'subjective', because with any luck we should be jolted into thinking more carefully about things we had hitherto taken for granted.

Here's an example. It is easy to be over-impressed by the differences between the language of the arts and the language of science. We all know that it is hard to translate poetry into other languages, but easy to translate scientific or mathematical statements (as long as the other language has suitable vocabulary). That is certainly a difference; we could call it the difference between personal and impersonal language. But just how impersonal do we think the scientific language is?

Gerald Hendrie, in the first music unit in this course, mentions a science-fiction novel called *The Black Cloud*, which is particularly concerned with the nature of communication between creatures of very different types (in this case, human beings and this cloud thing, which has no mouth, eyes or ears, but is sentient). A number of science-fiction novels toy with the problem of how such com-munication could be possible, and most of them make a very interesting assumption. One point which is usually assumed is that, if we are going to be able to communicate with an alien creature at all, there must be some common ground between us. Now *that* I would entirely agree with. But it is assumed *moreover* that this common ground will be in the mathematical/scientific area.

But this assumption embodies the conviction that there is nothing peculiarly *human* about our science and mathematics. The idea is that any creature whose race has enough science and mathematics to build itself a space craft (or get across space *some*how), must have enough of *the* science and mathematics, *our* science and mathematics, to provide us with some common ground.

Once this assumption is brought out into the open, it does not look completely obvious. Now we have had the startling thought 'The interpretation is *human*

18

interpretation', we can think again. Any creature whose race has enough science and mathematics to build itself a space craft must have some science and mathematics – obviously. But must it be like *our* science and maths.? It might be. But *must* it be?

You might say – well, what else could it be like? And of course I cannot say. I cannot describe, in human terms, using human concepts, something *completely* alien. But there might be such an alien science all the same.

If one thinks of science as objective, in contrast to the arts, it would be quite natural to take it for granted that there couldn't be an alien science or maths. And one could be jolted into thinking more carefully about this assumption if someone said, 'Science has a subjective element; it involves human interpretation.'

Here is another example. Someone might contrast the possibility of complete and final *proof* in science and mathematics with the impossibility of proof in the arts. But once we have had the thought 'Science involves human interpretation', the contrast does not seem so striking. Even in science and mathematics, certain things have to be accepted without proof, to serve as the basis for proving other things. The concepts of *proof* and *explanation* are, after all, two-termed. That is, you explain something in terms of something *else*, which is either understood, or itself in need of explanation. You prove something from something *else*, which is either already proved, or itself in need of proof, or accepted without proof. If there weren't some things which we just understood, if there weren't some things which we just accepted without proof, our proofs in science wouldn't get off the ground.[1] If some alien didn't just understand, and didn't accept the things we accept, if he (or it) just saw things differently, we wouldn't necessarily be able to prove him wrong.

So the shock value of 'subjective' *can* be useful – when people are over-impressed by the differences between science and the arts.

But there is not much point in our trying to shock the people who already think that science is subjective in the sense that scientists' judgements are inescapably biased, prejudiced, etc. To them, the idea of an alien science, and the idea that there might be more than one way of looking at things, is just old hat. So, whether you should say 'Science is objective' or 'Science is subjective' really depends on who you are talking to, what *they* think and what you think they will take you to be saying.

So what is the answer to the blanket question, 'Does science have a subjective element or doesn't it?' Please write your answer down.●

ANSWER

The answer *must* be 'It all depends what you mean by "subjective". There is a grain of truth both in saying it does and saying it doesn't, according to what you mean.'

If someone said to you, 'Science is subjective' or 'Science has a subjective element', what should you ask him? Please write your answer down.●

ANSWER

You should ask him, 'What do you mean?' or 'What do you mean by "subjective"?' Unfortunately, that does tend to receive the reply, 'Well, I meant what I said. Don't you understand plain English?' Fortunately there is another way to find out what someone means (or what he ought to mean) and that is to ask,

---

[1] This is a very difficult idea and I don't expect you to grasp it first time round. I introduce it here as something you can look back to. It comes up again, and is more thoroughly explored, in the next unit, and in Radio Programme 14, 'What the Tortoise said to Achilles.'

'Why do you say that? What are your grounds?' And then you can find out whether you seriously disagree (about, for instance, the nature of science, or what scientists do, or the possibility of final proof or . . .) or whether any disagreement you have is purely verbal (and merely hinges on attaching different senses to 'subjective').

1.7   REVISION OF THE TWO PRECEDING SECTIONS

As before, I shall give you a short summary of what has been said in the last two sections, and as before I shall first give you a set of questions such that if you answer them in complete and informative sentences, the summary will write itself. I shall begin by asking the *last* question of the previous revision section again, so you would be well advised to skip back and re-read that summary before starting on this one.

Here are the questions.

1   Should we, from the point that the facts do not speak for themselves, conclude simply, 'So science has a subjective element'?
2   How would 'Science has a subjective element' naturally be taken?
3   So why should we (unlike the Uri Geller supporters) not conclude, 'So science has a subjective element'?
4   Is 'biased, prejudiced, influenced by feelings, age and environment, etc.' the only meaning of the word 'subjective'?
5   What can 'subjective' also be used to mean?
6   Does 'Science has a subjective element' lose its shock value?
7   Can its shock value be useful?
8   What is the answer to the question, 'Does science have a subjective element?'?●

MY SUMMARY

(1)   From the point that the facts do not speak for themselves, we should not conclude simply and straightforwardly, 'So science has a subjective element', for (2) this would naturally be taken as making the dramatic claim that scientists cannot keep their feelings, biases and prejudices out of their science and hence (3) *we* shouldn't conclude, 'So science has a subjective element', because we would be misunderstood. (It's all right for the Geller supporters – they *do* mean what they would be taken to mean.) Of course (4) 'biased, prejudiced, influenced by feelings, age and environment, etc.' is not the only meaning of the word 'subjective' which (5) can also be used to mean, very generally, personal or human involvement of any sort. When 'subjective' is used in this sense (6) 'Science has a subjective element' does not lose its shock value, but this does not necessarily matter, since (7) its shock value can be useful in jolting us into thinking more carefully about things we had hitherto taken for granted, such as the difference between maths. and science and the arts. So (8) the answer to the question, 'Does science have a subjective element?' must be 'It all depends on what you mean by "subjective".'

2 SCEPTICISM

2.1   INTRODUCTION

Although I just allowed that there is a sense of 'subjective' in which it is true to say, 'Science has a subjective element', and although I allowed the shock value of this way of expressing the point to be useful, I did so with some reluctance. I am inclined to believe that one should *never* say, 'Science is subjective' because, once it is said, it is *so* hard to avoid the pull towards scepticism. One begins to think that science, in virtue of being 'subjective', does not provide us with real knowledge or real certainty.

> The gods did not reveal, from the beginning,
> All things to us; but in the course of time,
> Through seeking, men find that which is better.
> Let us conjecture that this is like truth.
> But as for certain truth, no man has known it,
> Nor will he know it; neither of the gods,
> Nor yet of all the things of which I speak.
> And even if by chance he were to utter
> The final truth, he would himself not know it;
> For all is but a woven web of guesses.[1]

We say that our science provides us with knowledge of the world – but how do we know? It is expressed by means of human concepts – how do we know they are the right ones? Within our science we can prove things, but the proofs have to be based on something; things assumed to be true. How do we know that those assumptions are right? When the answers to these (very difficult) questions do not come immediately to mind, it is quite easy to slide straight over into scepticism: we do not really know and all is but a woven web of guesses. And this brings us to the view which will be discussed in this part of the unit.

Figure 4   Socrates (pronounced Sock-ra-tease), 470/469–399 B.C., born in Athens where he spent most of his life, discussing philosophical topics. He wrote nothing himself and what we know of his philosophy comes to us mainly through the dialogues of Plato, in which he is frequently depicted as showing people that they don't know what they claimed to know. If you would like a bit of light relief in this course, read Mary Renault's novel The Last of the Wine, *which is about Athens in Socrates' time. It is a novel, but based on good sources*

[1] An imaginative translation of three fragments of Xenophanes. I copied it into the front of a book fifteen years ago from I know not now what source. My gratitude to the author, whoever he may be.

2.2   ORDINARY JUSTIFICATION

Philosophers have always been concerned with the question 'How do we know?' and from Socrates onwards have made themselves unpopular by pressing this question and demanding that people justify their most cherished beliefs. But traditionally, they have always demanded a rather peculiar sort of justification. Of course, it is not only philosophers who demand that claims to knowledge should be justified. Suppose we are in court:

Witness 1:   The accused was in his house at 4 p.m. on Tuesday.

Lawyer: How do you know?

Witness 1:   Well, he always is on Tuesday afternoons.

The jury knows that this isn't good enough. It leaves too much room for doubt. But suppose another witness says instead:

Witness 2:   Just after the wireless gave the time as ten to four, I went next door and rang the accused's bell; he answered and we had a long talk. As I came back into my own house the wireless said it was quarter past four.

Then the jury sees that his claim to knowledge is justified. There is surely now no room for doubt. (Except doubt about whether the witness is telling the truth.) The defence lawyer suggests hopefully that perhaps it was someone else in disguise, not the accused; perhaps the witness couldn't see too clearly . . . ? (Thus trying to raise a shadow of doubt.)

Lawyer: Are you absolutely certain?

But the witness says:

Witness 2:   I've known him for years; he was in front of me in full daylight; we talked, and I know his voice. I know it was him.

There is no point in the defence trying to break down that bit of evidence. It is beyond reasonable doubt.

Or we might have this dialogue:

Witness 1:   I know the victim was worried about being attacked.

Lawyer: How do you know?

Witness 1:   Well, what person wouldn't be? *I* was certainly worried, and I said to my wife at the time . . .

That witness will be asked to limit himself to the known facts. But we have another witness:

Witness 2:   I know the victim was worried about being attacked. He told me so many times; lost quite a lot of weight after the first threat, was looking strained, and I know he wanted police protection because he rang the police about it while I was there.

Once again, it is clear to everyone that the first claim to knowledge is not justified, but the second one is, beyond a shadow of reasonable doubt. You don't have to be any sort of specialist to see whether the question 'How do you know?' has been given a satisfactory answer. Given helpful hints from the lawyers and the judge, people in the jury don't find it difficult. We all know what ordinary justification is. In his units, Ossie Hanfling is relying on his reader's ability to judge when a conclusion has been adequately supported and when it hasn't. Of course, he's not assuming that we never make mistakes. But he is assuming, justifiably, that given a few helpful hints we will be able to agree whether a conclusion has been supported. He allows that we may disagree with *some* of his comments and counter-examples; that *some*times what seemed obvious to him won't seem obvious to us and vice versa. But if we didn't agree with him most of the time, and with each other, we wouldn't be able to talk about ordinary justification, or the supporting of conclusions at all. And most of the time we do agree.

2.3 THE PHILOSOPHICAL SCEPTIC

But the sceptic, notoriously, does *not* agree. What makes him so odd and so disturbing is that he is not satisfied with ordinary justification. Instead of accepting that the witness knows the accused was in, because he saw him and talked to him, the sceptic questions whether the witness can even be sure that there was a man to be seen or talked to at all. 'All you really know,' he says, 'is that you had certain visual and auditory sensations or sense-impressions – but how do you know, how do any of us know, that these sensations are caused by anything external? Macbeth thought he saw a dagger – but there was no dagger there. People with DT's think they see pink elephants (or is it rats?) – but there are none there. Even if the sensations *are* caused by something external, how can you know, how can any of us know, that what causes them is anything like what we think it is?'

The sceptic also questions the claim to know that the victim was worried. 'All you saw and heard,' he says, 'was the victim behaving in certain ways, and certain changes in his body. How do you know, how do any of us know, that he wasn't just pretending to be worried? Or even worse, how do you know there was anything going on in his mind at all? How do you know he *has* a mind? The only mind you are acquainted with is your own; you have never had experience of anyone else's. How do you know that yours isn't the only one?'

These two, very roughly sketched, lines of argument are known as scepticism about the external world and scepticism about other minds. We shall be going into the first one much more thoroughly in Unit 15; I don't expect you to make much sense of it at the moment. It is what I would call a real philosopher's problem – the sort of problem that people who are not inclined towards philosophy are irritated by – and I don't want to put you off straight away. But perhaps you will see what the sceptic is driving at in the case of the other-minds problem, because this *is* a philosophical problem which in some form or another occurs to quite a lot of people in ordinary life. It is a theme which often comes up in literature:

> . . . it was she who first gave me the idea that a person does not (as I had imagined) stand motionless and clear before our eyes with his merits, his defects, his plans, his intentions with regard to ourself exposed on his surface, like a garden at which, with all its borders spread out before us, we gaze through a railing, but is a shadow, which we can never succeed in penetrating, of which there can be no such thing as direct knowledge, with respect to which we form countless beliefs, based upon his words and sometimes upon his actions, though neither words nor actions can give us anything but inadequate and as it proves contradictory information – a shadow behind which we can alternately imagine, with equal justification, that there burns the flame of hatred and of love.[1]

The author is, in effect, speaking as a sceptic about our knowledge of other minds. It is as if he were saying, 'I have direct knowledge of my *own* intentions with regard to others, direct knowledge of my *own* feelings – *I* know whether I feel hatred or love – but, in contrast to this clear and certain knowledge I have of myself, how sketchy and incomplete, how dubious and never-to-be-confirmed, is my so-called knowledge of the minds of other people. How infinitely mysterious they are.' (NB. That is not what *I* say; it is what the sceptic about our knowledge of other minds says.)

Or one can think of the lack of knowledge as operating the other way:

> When I look at a red flag, my head turns, my eyes focus themselves at the proper distance, certain tensions and inhibitions are produced which I call 'paying attention' to it, incipient reactions of various sorts are engendered

---

[1] Marcel Proust, *A la recherche du temps perdu* (*Remembrance of Things Past*), trans. C. K. Scott Moncrieff, Chatto and Windus.

> . . . . All this is grist to the behaviourist's[1] mill. But *in addition* to all this, I have the sensation *red*. The behaviourist who is studying my reactions cannot find the sensation red anywhere in me . . . Nor can the behaviourist discover my feelings and emotions, my thoughts and my dreams. He can guess at them by studying my reactions; but the quality of my feelings eludes him. He may see me writhing, but he cannot feel my pain. He may see my smiles, measure my muscular tensions, count my heartbeats, discover what my glands are doing, but he cannot feel my happiness. That, and all the rest of my conscious experience, is private.[2]

Here the author is being sceptical about our knowledge of his mind. It is as if he were saying, 'You can only guess at my feelings by studying my reactions; I *know* my own feelings.' But of course that still leaves him with the other-minds problem. He must also say, 'I can only guess at your feelings by studying your reactions. I don't *know* them.' (Once again, let me emphasize that this is not what *I* say; it is what the sceptic about other minds says.)

The problem is sometimes made very vivid in science-fiction stories. I remember in particular, though I have not been able to track it down, a short story which consisted mostly of an ordinary love story. The narrator describes how he met his girlfriend, their early courtship, quarrels, making up, getting married, etc. The punch line comes at the end where, after a car accident, he discovers that his had not been a story of boy meets girl, but of boy meets robot! The implication of the story is that he thought he had understood ⌜her⌝ and had known what ⌜she⌝ was feeling; but he was wrong; ⌜she⌝ hadn't been feeling anything at all, but only behaving as though ⌜she⌝ did.

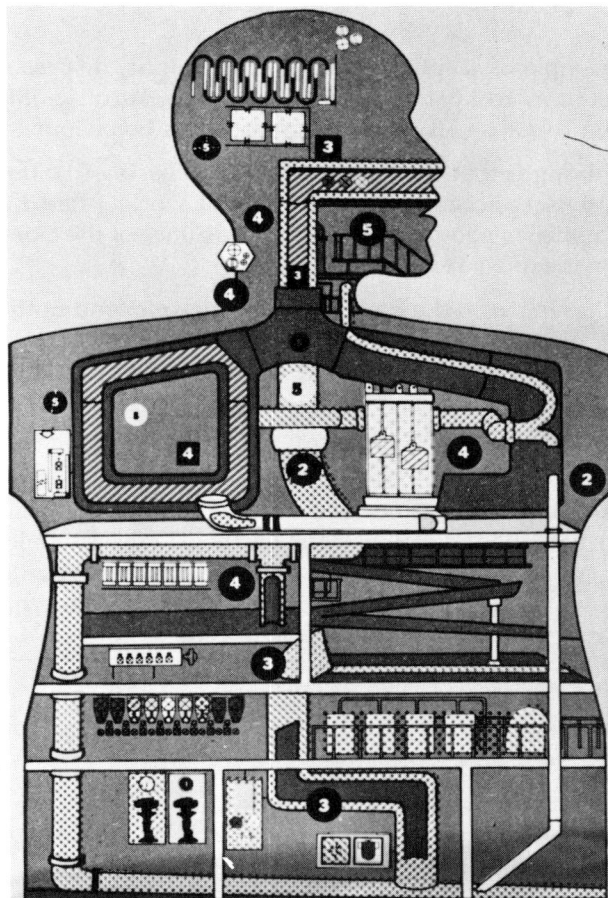

---

[1] A *behaviourist* is, roughly, someone who holds the thesis that mental phenomena – sensations, feelings, emotions, thoughts and dreams – just are pieces of behaviour.
[2] Durant Drake, *Invitation to Philosophy*, Houghton Mifflin, Boston.

I hope at least one of these examples, or some experience from your own life, will enable you to see the point of scepticism about other minds. What we have, in the case of assertions about other people's conscious experience, is a *gap* between what is asserted (e.g. 'the chap was worried') and the grounds, support or evidence for what is asserted, which is never anything better than a description of the person's behaviour. A sceptic is one who draws our attention to this gap, encouraging us to see it as a yawning abyss, rather than as something we can slide over easily.

Philosophers have discovered, or noticed, gaps in many other areas too, not just in the case of assertions about other people's conscious experience. I mentioned one area above, at the beginning of this section. The sceptic about our knowledge of the external world draws our attention to the gap between our assertions about the existence of things and events and the grounds, support or evidence for what is asserted which (according to him) is never anything better than a description of things within ourselves – our sensations.

Ossie Hanfling[1] gave examples of several areas where the philosophical sceptic claimed that we did not really know something we all thought was beyond doubt. They were (a) 'We cannot know what will happen tomorrow', (b) 'We can't really be certain what happened in the past', (c) 'I cannot know for certain that another person really feels pain', and (d) 'We cannot know that there is a chair in the next room if no-one is perceiving it.'

Are any of these examples of areas we have discussed already? Please write your answer down.●

ANSWER

Yes. (c) is an example of scepticism about other minds, discussed above. 'I can know for certain that *I* feel pain but I can only guess, surmise, infer that another person feels pain, because all I have to go on is his behaviour.'

You may have thought that we had just been discussing (d), but (d) is slightly different from the scepticism about the external world I had mentioned. One might call (d) scepticism about the persisting existence of the external world. For it is concerned with this gap:

Assertion: There is a chair in the next room, but no-one (and nothing) perceiving it.
Grounds: I saw it half a minute ago (and no-one has moved it).
That is, the assertion is about the *un*observed or *un*perceived but the grounds are about the observed (or perceived).

What about (a) and (b)? Can you see the gap between assertions about what will happen tomorrow (a) and our grounds for them? Between assertions about what happened in the past (b) and our grounds for them? Please would you do this as an exercise. First of all write down (a) an example of an assertion about what will happen tomorrow, and (b) an example of an assertion about what happened in the past. Not fancy examples – just simple ones.●

Of course I don't know what you have thought of; if you couldn't think of examples, use mine.

(a) *Assertion:* He's going to have an awful headache tomorrow.
(b) *Assertion:* Caesar conquered Gaul.
or: The stew was put on the stove an hour ago.

Now we want related examples of grounds for such assertions. Grounds are simply the reasons someone gives if he makes the assertion and someone says,

---

[1] Units 2B and 9, page 18.

'How do you know?' or 'What makes you think that?' So either for your own examples, or for mine, now write down the grounds. Once again, just simple; imagine an ordinary conversation.●

(a) *Grounds:* He's drinking such a lot; *or perhaps:* He has drunk such a lot.

(b) *Grounds:* There are some documents and archaeological evidence that prove it.

or: It's now bubbling away and nearly cooked.

And now try to make clear what the difference is between assertion and grounds in each case. For instance, what I said above was that the assertion in question is about the *un*observed or *un*perceived but the grounds are about the observed or perceived. If I wanted to make clear the gap between assertions about other minds and our grounds for them, I would say the assertion is about other *minds*, but the grounds are about only, or nothing but, the behaviour of other *bodies*. Or, to show the gap between assertions about external objects and the grounds for them, I would say the assertion is about an *ex*ternal object, independent of me, but the grounds are about only, or nothing but, my sensations, which are *not* external to, or independent of, me. So try to complete the following two sentences:

(a) The assertion is about the *future*, but the grounds are about nothing but . . .
(b) The assertion is about the *past*, but the grounds are about nothing but . . .●

SPECIMEN ANSWERS

(a) The assertion is about the *future* but the grounds are about nothing but the *present* or the *past*. E.g. my grounds for saying that he *will* have a headache *tomorrow* are that he *is* drinking such a lot *now*, in the *present*. Or, my grounds for saying that the sun *will* rise *tomorrow* are that it always *has* risen in the *past*.

(b) The assertion is about the *past* but the grounds are about nothing but what exists or is happening in the *present*. E.g. my grounds for saying that Caesar conquered Gaul are the *present* existence of certain documents and archaeological evidence. My grounds for saying that the stew *was* put on the stove an hour ago is that it is *now* bubbling away.

There is a special case of scepticism about the past which perhaps occurred to you, and that is scepticism about memory.

(b)' The assertion is about what I did or experienced in the *past*. My grounds are a *present* experience of mine, namely my having a memory-impression of having done or experienced whatever it was. (I have to say 'memory-impression'; if I say my grounds are that I *remember*, I beg the question.)[1] E.g. my grounds for saying that I *did* put the stew on the stove are that I *now* have a memory-impression of having done so.

You may wonder who 'the sceptic' I keep referring to is. Actually he is an imaginary philosopher, a sort of compound of all the philosophers who have questioned, and even all the philosophers who *might* question, our ordinary knowledge claims. There have been some very famous sceptics who have held the views and put forward the arguments attributed to 'the sceptic' but sometimes we say 'the sceptic says' or 'the sceptic's argument is' without having any particular *real* sceptic in mind. One extremely useful function that *the* imaginary sceptic performs is to get us thinking hard about knowledge. He questions whether we know that tables and chairs exist unperceived (say, in the next room); that they exist at all, or have the qualities we think they have; he throws doubt on our knowledge of other people's feelings and sensations, of the future,

---

[1] Cf Units 2B and 9, page 29.

the past, of casual processes, of general laws – and yet more besides. All these may be questioned and arguments can be put forward to support the view that we don't really know about any of these things at all.

2.4   TWO REACTIONS TO SCEPTICISM

People hearing these arguments for the first time usually fall into one of two camps. One is the camp of stubborn common sense when they say, 'But that's just silly. We *do* know that our sensations are caused by such things as tables and chairs; we *do* know they exist out there, and when we don't perceive them; we *do* know what they are like (what qualities they have). And we *do* know that people are people and not just robots; we often know for certain that someone else is in pain. We *do* know about the past and the future, and all the other things. No-one *really* doubts any of this, and there's no point in pretending to.'

The other is the camp of despair when they say, 'Good grief, that's right. Strictly speaking I don't really know there are tables and chairs and other people. I don't really know that other people feel pain. Of course I *believe* it all, but I don't really know it. It's just subjective opinion.'

Now I think there is something wrong with both these reactions. For the next few pages, after a bit of background stuff, I am going to argue against the people who fall into the latter camp. So what am I going to argue? (I'm going to argue that it's *not true* that . . .?)●

ANSWER

I'm going to argue that it's *not true* that we don't really know there are tables and chairs and other people. I'm going to argue that it's not true that we don't really know, not for certain, that other people feel pain.

If that is what I'm going to argue is *not* true, what must I be arguing *is* true? (This isn't a tricky question. It's just to make sure you can cope with all the negatives in the above answer.)●

ANSWER

I'm going to be arguing that (it is true that) we *do* really know there are tables and chairs and other people. I'm going to be arguing that we do really know, for certain, that other people feel pain.

But doesn't that mean that I agree with the people who fall into the common-sense camp? Aren't they just the people who said, 'The sceptic is wrong. We do know'? And if I agree, why did I say there was something wrong with *both* reactions, instead of just saying it was wrong to fall into the camp of despair and agree with the sceptic?

Well, I probably do agree with some people in the common-sense camp. But I know there is a difference between me and some people there, which is that I can *justify* my claim to know that the sceptic is wrong and they can't. I'm going to produce an *argument* against the sceptic and say, 'You are wrong because . . .' Now until you can do that, you should not, in *this* context, claim to know that the sceptic is wrong.

So if you are gripped by scepticism and think that strictly speaking we don't really know that there are tables and chairs, or that other people have feelings and so on: read on and I hope I can convince you that we *do* really know.[1] And if

---

[1] I don't *expect* I shall. It took me five years to shake off scepticism. But I still needed to learn the argument.

you are convinced already, read on and learn how to argue in support of your convictions.

(What is special about *this* context, which I mentioned in the second to last paragraph? *This* is the philosophical context. As Ossie Hanfling pointed out,[1] we do in fact, and quite rightly, make many assertions without giving reasons, and I am certainly not encouraging you to raise sceptical doubts about our knowledge of the past in the context of doing history, and then claim to know that the sceptic is wrong and produce an argument against him and *then* (*only* then) start doing the history. Of course normally we don't have to worry about showing that the sceptic is wrong. But arguing against the sceptic is part of philosophical tradition. It's one of the things you learn to do when you learn to philosophize.)

2.5   DESCARTES AND THE METHOD OF DOUBT

René Descartes (pronounced Day-Cart), 1596–1650, was a French philosopher who is often referred to as the father of modern philosophy. There are many reasons for giving him this title; *one* of them is that although he was certainly not the first sceptic, he is the philosopher who made the sceptical way of thinking famous and introduced the method of doubt. He decided

to reject *as if* absolutely false anything as to which I could *imagine* the least doubt, *in order to* see if I should not be left at the end believing something that was absolutely indubitable.

Figure 5   René Descartes (1596–1650)

[1] Units 2B and 9, page 12.

(Notice the italics; they are mine, not Descartes'.) This is the method of doubt. Can you see, from this very short passage, whether the method requires that we actually get ourselves into the psychological state of doubt? Does it require that we actually make ourselves believe that, for example, it's false that there is a world around us? What do you think? Don't worry if you think the passage doesn't make it clear. Just read on.●

I don't know whether it *is* clear from the passage on its own, but it is clear from other passages that Descartes' method does *not* require that we really make ourselves doubt. We reject *as if* false our belief in, for example, the world around us. We do not have to doubt it ourselves; only *imagine* the least doubt. So, for instance, you imagine that someone, anyone, even a madman, casts doubt on something you believe and see if you can *prove* to him that you are right. And if you can't, then you put that belief on one side for the moment; reject it *as if* false, however certain you, personally, still feel about it.

Following this method, Descartes allowed himself to entertain the most weird and wonderful hypotheses. Perhaps his senses were deceiving him and there wasn't a pen in his hand or paper in front of him. Perhaps he didn't even have a hand, or legs, or a backside on a chair. Perhaps there was nothing in the universe except his mind and an evil demon who was spitefully deluding him into thinking he had a body and that it was resting on a chair and pushing pen over paper. Perhaps there wasn't even an evil demon. Perhaps there was nothing in the universe except himself, his mind, dreaming.

Remember, it is not disputed that these are the wildest fantasies. They are not being offered for serious consideration and *they* do not call for proof. You are not allowed to say, 'You prove to me that my senses are deceiving me; you prove to me that I don't have a body, or that I am dreaming.' The onus of proof falls on the other side. 'You prove that your senses *aren't* deceiving you, you prove you *do* have a body; you prove that you *aren't* dreaming. And if you can't, put the belief on one side for a moment.'

What, you may ask, is the point of this procedure? Descartes told us what he thought the point was. Please would you look back at the quotation and see if you can spot it. (This *is* clear in the passage, I think.)●

ANSWER

The point for Descartes is: 'To see if I should not be left at the end believing something that was absolutely indubitable.' The next question is: And what is the point of finding something absolutely indubitable? The point of doing that, for Descartes and indeed for many other philosophers, is that for them it is finding the proper foundation for a system of knowledge. Descartes would say a system of knowledge should, after all, be built on rock, not on sand, otherwise it does not count as a system of knowledge at all, but only of more or less probable opinion (subjective again). As you will hear in the radio programme associated with this unit, the need for *one*, indubitably based, system of knowledge was particularly biting in Descartes' day, when, for the first time, physical science was ceasing to be part of philosophy and was developing its own techniques for giving a reasoned account of the nature of the world. Unfortunately the techniques of the astronomers Copernicus, Kepler and Galileo led them to conclusions incompatible with the teachings of the Church. Both sides could not be right, but Descartes was not prepared to dismiss either side as obviously wrong. A real system of knowledge should make it possible to assess the competing claims of both sides and extract the truth from both.

Descartes' model of what a real system of knowledge ought to look like was provided by Euclidean geometry. There you had a small number of basic assertions made without reasons; these were *axioms* which were apparently absolutely indubitable. You also had a small number of definitions which were true *by* definition, and on the basis of these and the axioms, you built up a whole system. You derived new theorems from the axioms and definitions by rigorous mathematical reasoning; those theorems, *once proved*, inherited the indubitability of the axioms and definitions, and you could then use them for proving yet more. And so on.

Descartes intended to apply the same method to ordinary non-mathematical knowledge. He said in a letter:

> If you have a basket of apples, some of which (as you know)[1] are bad and will spoil and poison the rest, you have no other means than to empty your basket completely and then take and test the apples one by one, in order to put the good ones back in your basket and throw away those that are not.

The way in which you test the apples of knowledge, as it were, is by applying the method of doubt to them. Any that pass the test go into the basket as absolutely indubitable and become the axioms. Those that remain are put through the test of proof. Can they be derived, with mathematical rigour, from the indubitable ones in the basket? If so, they go into the basket too and can be used as a basis for proving others. Those that can't, remain outside (rejected *as if* false), awaiting conclusive proof or disproof.

The intricacies of the way in which Descartes filled up *his* basket and constructed *his* system of knowledge, the mistakes he made, the unquestioned and highly questionable axioms he smuggled in (without noticing) to reach the conclusions he wanted to reach – these need not concern us here. What we need to note is two things. *One* is the special sort of justification Descartes demanded of a claim to knowledge:

Ordinary man: I know there are tables and chairs.

Descartes: How do you know?

Ordinary man: I see them, I feel them.

Descartes: That's not enough. *Prove* it, in such a way that their existence is absolutely guaranteed. I say that they are possibly hallucinatory. Prove to me that it's logically impossible that they are hallucinatory. Prove their existence to me from indubitable premises and definitional truths by methods of pure logic. Prove it in such a way that you can't be wrong. And don't claim to know they exist until you have.

The second thing we should notice is that it was not crazy of *Descartes* to demand this special sort of justification for claims to knowledge, because *he* believed that it was possible to find it. Descartes never expected that we should all finish up saying, 'Good grief, strictly speaking I don't know there are tables and chairs; strictly speaking I don't know there are other minds.' He expected that we would wind up justifiably claiming to know most of the things we ordinarily claim to know – *when* we had proved them rigorously from the indubitable premises. To put it in terms of his own metaphor, he was not intending to throw out nearly all the apples. He expected that we should wind up with a basket almost as full as it had been before, just minus a few rotten ones.

This is an important point, and it is worth our while making sure you have got hold of it. Suppose someone claims to know something; suppose *you* know that there is a proper justification of what he claims to know but – he can't give it! Do you agree with him that he knows, or do you tell him not to claim to know until or unless he can produce the proper justification?●

---

[1] You know some must be bad because you are getting contradictory results. E.g. *something* said by the astronomers or the Church must be false because what they each say leads to contradictory conclusions – that the earth does (or does not) move.

ANSWER

I would tell him he doesn't know. I would say, 'Yes, you are *right*. But it's just a lucky guess on your part. You are not in a position to claim to *know* unless you can produce better grounds than the ones you gave.' Try to think of an example of someone being right, and claiming to know, but not being justified in claiming to know. If you haven't thought of one of your own in two minutes, turn back to pp. 22–23 and see if they suggest one to you.●

ANSWER

Pages 22–23 were the ones on which I discussed the two witnesses, and they would provide us with an example. The first witness claims to know the accused was in; as we learn from the second witness, he was right. The accused *was* in, but the first witness didn't really know that. He knew that the accused was usually in on Tuesday afternoons and he made a reasonable bet. The first witness claimed to know the victim was worried. Although he was right, he didn't *know*. He had made a very reckless generalization which, quite fortuitously, turned out to apply to this case. In each case, a justification of what the first witness claims to know *can* be given, and *is* given by the second witness who, we say, *does* know.

Even if there were no second witness, we would still agree that there *is* a proper justification for claims such as 'I know he was in at 4 pm.' or 'I know he was worried.' If no-one can give this proper justification, then no-one knows whether the accused was in, or the victim worried.

Demanding that people give the proper justification is also our check on people repeating things parrot fashion. A child says, 'History is subjective.' 'How do you know?' we say. If he says, 'Well, that's what my teacher says anyhow,' and can't tell us anything else, then we say he doesn't know what he's talking about.

Another example you might have picked up out of the text is my objection to some people in the common-sense camp. You shouldn't say you know the sceptic is wrong unless you can answer the question '*How* do you know?' Perhaps with some things there is no answer to this question but 'We just *do* know'; but this isn't one of them. There are arguments against the sceptic's position; there is a justification for claiming to know that the sceptic is wrong and until you can produce justification, you shouldn't say you *know*.

Descartes, in effect, told us that we shouldn't claim to know the things we ordinarily claim to know, *because* ordinarily we didn't give the proper sort of justification. He thought the proper sort of justification would consist of a proof of mathematical rigour from indubitable premises and he thought this was possible: that there *was* such a justification for most of the things we ordinarily claim to know. He thought our ordinary justification ('I see and feel the tables and chairs') was like the child's 'Teacher told me', or the witness's 'Well, he always *is* in then, isn't he?', or the common-sense 'Well, the sceptic just *is* wrong.' It was some justification, but very little; certainly not enough to support a claim to know; a long way from the ⌐proper⌐ justification which would prove the matter conclusively and indubitably.

You will notice I have just put scare quotes around 'proper'. This is to make quite clear that *I* am not saying, 'The proper justification would prove the matter conclusively and indubitably.' Descartes was quite wrong in thinking that there was a fail-safe sort of justification, a sort which would prove the matter conclusively and indubitably. But given that he *did* think it, he was doing something sensible. Just as the lawyer said to the witness, as we say to the child, as I say to the people in the common-sense camp, so he was saying to us, 'There is a proper justification, and you haven't given it yet, and you shouldn't claim to know until you can produce it.' *That's* perfectly sensible.

2.6 THE MODERN SCEPTIC

You may feel that I have laboured this point, but it is important to grasp the distinction between this *sensible* 'You don't really know' and the sort that is *not* sensible.

Suppose Descartes says to me, 'You don't really know (that there are tables and chairs for instance)'. I might turn on him, putting the ball back in his court, and say, 'How do you *know* I don't really know?' (Remember, asking 'How do you know?' is often a way of finding out what someone means.) Well, Descartes has a reply. 'You don't really know,' he says, 'because you don't give the proper justification. You justify your claim to know by mentioning no more than your senses. But there's a better justification than that. And until you give that fail-safe justification you shouldn't claim to know.'Descartes has *grounds* for saying, 'You don't really know.'

Contrast that with the following. Suppose you have someone who realizes that not everything can be proved by mathematics and logic. Suppose you have someone who realizes that Descartes was wrong in thinking that statements about tables and chairs and other minds could ever be infallibly derived from indubitable premises. What does he say? 'There is no better justification than the ordinary one; you couldn't produce anything better than the ordinary one, but you shouldn't claim to know until you can produce something that can't be produced. And that means that, except for a very few absolutely indubitable things, you shouldn't claim to know anything at all.'

I would say that *that* doesn't sound sensible at all. But in effect, that is what the modern sceptic says. Bertrand Russell, for instance, writing in 1912, concluded

Figure 6 Bertrand Russell (1872–1970), drawn by Vicky

that 'the greater part of what would commonly pass as knowledge is more or less probable opinion'. It is the mark of what I have called the modern sceptic that, *unlike* Descartes, he does *not* think there is some special fail-safe form of justification which could be produced to back up our ordinary claims to knowledge. But *like* Descartes, he says our ordinary justifications are not good enough. So he winds up saying that except for a very few absolutely indubitable things, which pass Descartes' first test, we shouldn't claim to know anything at all. We should throw out nearly all the apples.

(Do you perhaps think that there must be a fail-safe sort of justification, as Descartes believed? Well, let's just think about it for a minute. When we try to imagine what the justification would look like in *detail*, doesn't the whole idea seem pretty implausible? Since most of our assertions are *not* mathematical or logical assertions, how could they appear suddenly at the end of a logical or mathematical proof? And remember that Descartes was intending that nearly *all* our knowledge should be justified along these lines. What *sort* of rigorous proof, from what sort of logically indubitable premises, could yield a conclusion about – the structure of the solar system, the sort of life on Mars, the colouring on a Red Admiral butterfly, or the digestive system of a cow? (To mention four things chosen at random.))

I have said that the modern sceptic does not sound sensible and I hope you agree with me that it is not sensible to say, 'You shouldn't claim to know until you have produced something that can't be produced.' But if he is not sensible, why does anyone ever fall for scepticism?

In part, one falls for scepticism because the point that there is nothing *better* than the ordinary justification is not emphasized. What *is* emphasized is how many holes can be shot in the ordinary justification, and this can give one such a shock that one fails to notice that it holds up despite all the holes. Some people are particularly struck by the thought that nothing ⌐*guarantees*⌐ that our interpretations of the facts are ⌐the right⌐ ones. I certainly was – that's why I used to say, 'Science is subjective.' If you had asked me, I wouldn't have been able to say what I meant by 'subjective', nor would I have been able to say what a guarantee that our interpretation was the right one could possibly be like. I didn't even have much idea what I meant by 'the right one'. (The only one? So that the Martians, or other creatures from outer space would agree? I hadn't really thought.)

The sceptic's questionings of our ordinary justifications can be so startling that, without even waiting to see whether we can patch things up a little, we can slide into scepticism. It is quite easy to go along with Bertrand Russell and other modern sceptics, agreeing with them that the only things we should claim to know are the statements of immediate experience (such as 'I *seem* to see a table' – nothing reckless about actually seeing a real one) and the truths of logic and mathematics. These apparently pass Descartes' first test; nothing else is known *or can be*, and out go nearly all the apples. To stay.

As I said earlier, I think that it is a mistake to slide into scepticism, but before I go on to the next section, we had better have some recapitulation. I think the last few pages have been rather dense and difficult. As before, would you please *either* write a 200-word (approx.) summary of the last two sections ('Descartes and the Method of Doubt', and 'The Modern Sceptic') *or* answer the following questions in complete and informative sentences, in which case the summary should write itself.

1   What was Descartes' method of doubt?
2   What was its point?
3   And what was the point of doing *that*?
4   How did Descartes expect to build up his system of knowledge?
5   Did he think our ordinary claims to knowledge were justified?
6   Did he think they could be justified?
7   So did he expect that eventually we would wind up rejecting most of our ordinary knowledge as mere opinion?

8 _Does the modern sceptic think our ordinary claims to knowledge are justified?

9 Does the modern sceptic think they can be given a better justification?

10 So what does *he* conclude about most of our ordinary knowledge?●

MY SUMMARY

(1) Descartes' method of doubt was to reject *as if* false anything as to which he could imagine the least doubt. (2) The point of this procedure was to find something absolutely indubitable which (3) would provide the secure rock-like foundation for a system of knowledge. According to Descartes (4) this system would be built up like Euclidean geometry: from the absolutely indubitable axioms, theorems would be proved with mathematical and logical rigour and these would provide a base for proving more. (5) Descartes thought our ordinary claims to knowledge were *not* justified because we did not ordinarily produce this sort of rigorous proof whereas (6) he thought such a proof could be given as proper justification of most of our ordinary knowledge. That is, (7) he expected that we would eventually wind up *not* rejecting most of our ordinary knowledge as mere opinion, but as claiming to know it with proper, indubitable justification. He was hence very different from the modern sceptic who, while (8) agreeing with Descartes that our ordinary claims to knowledge are not justified, (9) says that they cannot be given any better justification than the sort ordinarily given, and concludes (10) that we must reject most of our ordinary knowledge as mere opinion.

2.7   A GENERAL ARGUMENT AGAINST THE SCEPTIC

The modern sceptic is the philosopher who says that we don't know most of the things we think ordinarily that we do know. But we all go round saying that we do. We go round saying things like, 'There is a book on the desk; the victim was worried; I put the dinner on; etc.,' and if asked, 'Do you know that for certain?' we often say, 'Yes.' Should we all be saying something else instead?

In a way, this seems to be what the sceptic is suggesting. He seems to be recommending that we throw out our ordinary everyday ⌐loose⌐ use of the verb 'to know' and introduce a new strict use. It's as if he were saying, 'Let's use the word in a really narrow way. Let's keep it just for, e.g., the truths of logic and the statements of immediate experience. Let's not say, "I know there's a book on the table in front of me"; let's say instead, "Probably there's a book in front of me." Perhaps we should stick to "There's a book in front of me" but we should always add "possibly hallucinatory" or "but perhaps I'm dreaming" or . . . And when people ask us if we know we should say, "No, I'm merely of the opinion that . . .".'

But think what would happen if we did start talking this way. Ordinarily, phrases like 'probably . . .', 'possibly hallucinatory', 'perhaps I'm dreaming', 'No, I don't know, I am merely of the opinion that . . .' function as doubt-raisers. Ordinarily, we use them to mark the differences between the cases where they *are* appropriate, because there's room for reasonable doubt, and the other cases where it is appropriate to say, ordinarily, 'I know'.

Consider these examples. (As soon as you feel you understand, start trying to invent your own examples.)

(a)   If I know that I've just taken LSD, if I know that I have a fever, if I know that I have DT's, is it appropriate to claim to know that there is something peculiar like a pink mouse in front of me? No it's appropriate to disclaim knowledge and say, 'Possibly hallucinatory.' But if I'm undrugged, in perfect health, and ⌐seem⌐ to see and touch a brown mouse, that's a different set-up. *Then* it's appropriate to claim to know.

(b) If I'm in Madame Tussaud's (the waxwork place), is it appropriate to claim to know that there is a (real) doorman standing by the door? No, it's appropriate to say, 'Probably that's a real doorman . . .' But if we are in an ordinary theatre or hotel, that's a different set-up. Then it's appropriate to claim to know.

(c) If I am slightly acquainted with someone but know nothing about his health or private life and have never had a conversation with him about personal matters, is it appropriate to claim to know that he was worried? No, it's appropriate to say, 'No, I don't know, I am merely of the opinion that . . .' But if I am his best friend, have known him for years and he *told* me: then it's appropriate to claim to know.

And so on. If we give up our ordinary use of 'I know' and use the strict one instead, how are we to continue to mark these differences – the differences between the cases where I used to be allowed to say 'I know', because I had the best possible justification, and the cases where I used to have to say 'probably' or 'possibly hallucinatory' or 'I am of the opinion that . . .'? How are we to distinguish between the witness who does (as we now say) know that the accused was in, or the victim worried, and the witnesses who don't? How are we to distinguish between the (as we now say) known facts such as that Caesar conquered Gaul or that a cow has four stomachs, and the (as we now say) unknown ones, such as what Caesar had for breakfast on the Ides of March and the (as we now say) probable but not yet known ones, such as that smoking causes lung cancer? The sceptic does not deny that there *are* distinctions here. (Or if he does deny it, he has not yet produced his argument. Saying that all these cases are alike in that they fail to pass Descartes' first test is not proving that they are all alike as far as ordinary justification goes.)

So how, talking the new way, with the strict use of 'know', shall we mark these distinctions? It looks as though we should have to introduce a new word, *a word that would serve exactly the same function* as our old use of 'know'. Well, we could, but it seems unnecessarily elaborate. Why don't we keep our old use of 'know' and let the sceptic introduce a new word for his special strict sense?

But if he has to introduce a new word he will not manage to sound so revolutionary. When he uses 'know' and says, 'We don't know there are tables and chairs, that other people have feelings, we don't know what happened in the past or what will happen tomorrow', he trades on its *ordinary* use and makes it sound as though your belief that there is a book in front of you is as groundless as the drugged person's belief that there is a pink mouse in front of him. It makes it sound as though your belief that some person other than yourself wrote this unit and had these thoughts is as groundless as the child's belief that some person (i.e. the tooth fairy) other than its mother replaced the tooth under its pillow with a sixpence. Our beliefs about what happened in the past or what will happen in the future are made to sound like the reckless claims of pseudo-scientists to know about prehistoric man, or the future of the universe: as if we hadn't a shred of decent evidence for them. Ordinary 'know' contrasts with 'merely believes', 'has unjustified faith in', 'has the crackpot idea that . . .', 'is of the personal opinion that', and we all know what mere belief, unjustified faith, crackpot ideas and personal opinions are like. And one reason why the sceptic sounds so revolutionary is that he sounds as though he is telling us that what we all thought was knowledge is really like that – like the beliefs of children, crackpots, the prejudiced and biased, the drugged.

Perhaps that is a bit of an exaggeration. Admittedly the sceptic usually says, 'We don't *really* know' or 'Strictly speaking, we don't know' rather than 'We don't know at *all*.' But then he trades on the ordinary use of 'really know' and 'strictly speaking', and makes it sound as though we were *always* recklessly claiming to know on grounds that would not stand up in a court of law – as the first witnesses did.

It is true that we do make knowledge claims very casually in everyday conversation. 'Do you know where my old jeans are?' 'Yes, they're in the top

36

left-hand drawer.' Someone might say that, on the grounds that they had seen the jeans in that drawer three days ago. No-one bothers to question it under ordinary circumstances; but a witness who claimed to know that the murder weapon was in a certain drawer on a certain day, on the grounds that he had seen it there three days previously, would be pulled up sharply. Strictly speaking he doesn't know it was there on the day in question. It is reasonable for him to believe it was there, but he doesn't *really* know. The one who really knows is the one who saw it there on the day in question.

Not *all* our knowledge claims are casual, and made on grounds that would not stand up in a court of law. But that they are all equally casual, that 'strictly speaking' we don't know any of the things we ordinarily claim to know, that there is nothing to choose between the two witnesses, is just the dramatic thing that the sceptic seems to be saying. No wonder he sounds revolutionary and startling.

(This might remind you of the earlier discussion of the claim 'Science is subjective.' Saying that makes it *sound* as though scientific truths were as much a matter of personal emotional response as poetic ones. That is certainly dramatic, and no wonder the people who say 'Science is subjective' sound revolutionary and startling. But of course the dramatic claim is false.) Is the sceptic saying anything true? He says, 'We don't really know, strictly speaking we don't know, all those things we ordinarily claim to know', and he *doesn't* mean that we never give an ordinary justification for our claims (which would be false), and he *doesn't* mean that there's a fail-safe justification that we ought to give (which would be false), and he *doesn't* mean that our beliefs are like those of crackpots and children (which would be false), and he *doesn't* mean that all our knowledge claims are made casually on grounds that would not stand up in a court of law – which would be false. He shouldn't rely (as people sometimes do rely) on the phrase 'strictly speaking', or the more commonly relied-on 'philosophically speaking', as performing a sort of magic which turns nonsense into sense, or a false statement into a true one. If 'We don't know most of the things we ordinarily claim to know' is false, it remains false when someone puts 'philosophically speaking' in front of it. No-one could get away with 'Yes, yes, of course two and two make four, but *philosophically* speaking they make five.'[1]

So it seems hard to find anything that the sceptic means which is true. And yet, he seemed to have something. . .

I pointed out earlier that if you ask someone in this sort of context, 'What do you mean?' you are likely to get the reply, 'I meant what I said; don't you understand plain English?', *but* (I added) you can often find out what someone means, or what his claim boils down to, by asking him for his grounds. So instead of asking the sceptic, 'What do you mean?' we'll ask him what his grounds are for saying that we don't really know all those things we thought we did know.

If we do ask him this, his reply makes it clear that he *was* on to something, but it is not something about *knowledge*. His grounds are that most of the truths we ordinarily claim to know do not pass Descartes' first test. This is true, and possibly interesting, and is a remark about the logical status of those truths, but nothing as yet follows about what can or can't be known.

Let's remind ourselves about what Descartes and the modern sceptic had in common. They both reject as if false anything as to which they can imagine the least doubt. The point of this procedure is to arrive at truths which are logically indubitable (if there are any), truths that not even a madman could doubt, truths such that, if someone claimed to doubt them, we would not even understand him. This was Descartes' first test.

---

[1] In Television Programme 14, 'Jumpers', you will see this move mercilessly parodied. One character asks about someone else, incredulously, 'He thinks there's nothing *wrong* with *killing* people!?!' and the philosopher, unwilling to ascribe this psychopathic view to his harmless colleague, says, in some embarrassment, 'Well, put like that, of course . . . But *philosophically*, he doesn't think it's actually, inherently wrong in itself, no.' The first character is, rightly, amazed.

According to both Descartes and the modern sceptic, most of the truths we ordinarily claim to know do not pass this test. So far, this is just a distinction between two different sorts of truths – there are those that are logically indubitable and *do* pass Descartes' test – call these 'Cartesian truths' for the moment – and those that do *not*, e.g. truths about tables and chairs, other minds, the past, the future, etc.

Now, does simply drawing this distinction – between Cartesian and non-Cartesian truths – commit someone to drawing the conclusion that only *Cartesian* truths are known? Well, Descartes didn't draw that conclusion. Can you see any reason why anyone should?

You might say, fairly enough, that you don't know until you know more about Cartesian truths. It is easy to give examples of truths that do not pass Descartes' first test but not at all easy to give examples of truths that do. Both before and after Descartes, philosophers have been interested in what I am calling Cartesian truths, that is, logically indubitable truths. There has been debate over which statements *are* Cartesian truths, and different accounts of by virtue of what a statement does pass Descartes' first test. Perhaps the most traditional candidates have been mathematical statements; not only the arithmetic ones such as '2 + 2 = 4' but also the ones that somehow seem more illuminating, such as the definitions in geometry (a straight line is the shortest distance between two points), and/or less a matter of definition, such as 'Everything that has volume has shape.' Descartes himself plumped for 'I think, therefore I am', and, in thus emphasizing introspective experience, led other philosophers to concentrate on what are called statements of immediate experience such as 'I *seem* to see a white page in front of me' (nothing reckless and dubitable about actually seeing one).

Those are some possible candidates for Cartesian truths. If you think they look like a very ill-assorted bunch, you are in good company – many philosophers would agree with you. If you are beginning to have doubts about whether there really are any Cartesian truths at all, you are also in good company – some philosophers have argued that the very concept of Cartesian truths is an illusion and based on a muddle.

But the point is you could think about these things, and argue about the examples, without saying anything about *knowledge*. Whether or not a truth is a Cartesian truth, nothing follows immediately about whether or not it can or can't be (really) known.

Suppose that you and I *agree* with the sceptic that most of the truths we ordinarily claim to know do not pass Descartes' first test, i.e. are not Cartesian truths. (I certainly agree, don't you?) Well, so what? What follows?

What we think follows depends on what we think about Cartesian truths. If we think there aren't any anyhow, that nothing passes Descartes' first test, then there is nothing terribly interesting about pointing out that amongst all those truths that fail to pass it are the ones we ordinarily claim to know. Or suppose we have a theory about Cartesian truths; suppose we think that what makes a statement a Cartesian truth is its being true in virtue of the meanings of the words involved – Cartesian truths pass the test because if you try to deny them you contradict yourself. So if that is what Cartesian truths are, and most truths we ordinarily claim to know are different, then most truths we ordinarily claim to know are *not* true in virtue of the meanings of the words involved. From such a theory we might eventually evolve a theory of knowledge – but there is no reason to suppose it will involve the view that we only know the Cartesian truths. Indeed, we could imagine someone arguing that knowledge of Cartesian truths isn't really *knowledge* at all, but a sort of verbal expertise!

Don't worry about trying to understand the theories. Just consider the point that from the premise that most of the truths we ordinarily claim to know are not Cartesian truths, nothing follows straightforwardly about *knowledge*. Before anything follows, something has to be said about the Cartesian truths.

Summary of this section so far: The sceptic claims that we don't know most of the truths we ordinarily claim to know. If we interpret what he says straightforwardly he seems to be saying a whole lot of *false* things about knowledge: he seems to be denying the existence of the distinctions we usually mark by contrasting knowledge with probable opinion, reasonable belief, unreasonable belief, crackpot faith; or the distinction we mark by contrasting really knowing, strictly speaking, with not really knowing, strictly speaking (i.e. one couldn't swear to it in a court of law). He seems to be denying that these distinctions exist and asserting *falsely* that all these cases are alike. But saying that all the cases are alike in that they fail to pass Descartes' first test is not proving that they are all alike as far as ordinary justification goes. However, in saying that all these cases are alike in that they fail to pass Descartes' first test, the sceptic *is* saying something true. But it is not about knowledge, nor does it provide adequate grounds for saying anything about what can or can't be known.

At this point people are sometimes seized with another thought. 'But if most of the things we ordinarily claim to know don't pass Descartes' first test, then most of the things we claim to know are not logically indubitable. Only the Cartesian truths are truths which logically cannot be doubted, so they are the only truths about which you can be absolutely certain. We can't be absolutely certain about most of the things we ordinarily claim to know.'

I said that this was 'another thought'. Actually, it's not. It's the same thought with the trivial verbal difference of the substitution of 'absolutely certain' for 'know'. And faced with 'We can't be absolutely certain about most of the things we ordinarily claim to know', I shall run exactly the same sort of argument as I ran on 'I know.' Can you see how the argument will go? Try to write down a couple of sentences sketching it – perhaps giving the example or context you think I will use, or the phrases that I shall introduce.●

Are you absolutely certain?   *No*   *Yes*

It goes like this: 'I am absolutely certain' has an ordinary use in which it is contrasted with 'I am pretty certain', 'quite certain', 'not very certain', 'pretty unsure', 'not certain at all, just guessing' and so on. Back to our witnesses.

Witness 1:   He was in at four p.m.

Lawyer: Are you absolutely certain?

Witness 1:   Yes.

Lawyer: Why?

Witness 1:   Because he's always in at four on Tuesdays.

Lawyer: No, you should have said 'Quite certain' or 'Not entirely certain'. Next witness:

Witness 2: He was in at four.

Lawyer: Are you absolutely certain?

Witness 2: Yes.

Lawyer: Why?

Witness 2: Because just before I went over to speak to him I heard the radio say it was 3.50 and he came to the door . . ., etc.

If I can't have 'absolutely certain' to single out the occasions on which I have the best possible justification for what I assert, how can I mark the distinction between *those* cases and the other cases in which my evidence, though not the best possible, is good, is only fair, is minimal, and is non-existent? If I give you 'absolutely certain' for the exclusive use of the Cartesian truths, then I'll have to use 'nearly absolutely certain' where I used to use 'absolutely certain'. And so I'll need something else to replace the old use of 'nearly absolutely certain', such as 'pretty certain', but then I'll need something else . . . and so on down the line. Well, that's too complicated. I'll keep 'absolutely certain' and *you* introduce a new term.

I hope that by now I have convinced some of you that we don't need a new term. The *only* purpose it could serve is to single out Cartesian truths, and we don't need a new term to do that. We already have 'Cartesian truths', or we could use 'logically indubitable'. Or we could use the long, but adequate, description, 'truths-which-pass-Descartes'-first-test'.

You will find this argument re-iterated in the extract from J. Wisdom in the *Supplementary Texts*. If your study time is well in hand and you feel you are understanding the unit you should certainly read the Wisdom. If you are feeling muddled you could look at Wisdom in case you find him clearer than me, but if you find him as, or more, confusing, *don't* spend time on it. You would do better re-reading the unit.

2.8   THE VALUE OF SCEPTICISM

I said earlier that if you clung to the line of plain common sense and said, 'But we *do* know; we *are* absolutely certain; it's silly of the sceptic to deny this', you should still read through my attack on the sceptic in order to learn *how* to attack him. Learning philosophy is, in part, acquiring a technique, the technique of argument. Let's suppose that we have now completed our argument against the sceptic and are justified in claiming to know that he is wrong. That puts us one step ahead of the position of plain common sense. It is not enough to be right; one has to learn to argue for one's position.

But the matter does not end there, for the sceptic himself does not simply assert dogmatically, 'You don't know there are tables and chairs and other minds, etc.' *He* produces an argument for *his* position. He says, for example, 'You don't know there are tables and chairs *because* all you perceive are your own sensations; for all you know there is nothing that causes them or corresponds to them.' Or he says, 'You don't know there are other minds *because* the only one you are acquainted with is your own; all you are acquainted with apart from that are certain bodies behaving in certain ways: for all you know they are nothing but robots.' Sceptical philosophers have produced *arguments* against the possibility of knowing about the past, the future, causality, right and wrong; practically anything you can think of.

Of course the arguments are much more complicated than I have indicated. Those are mere sketches. But in each case we do have an *argument* whose conclusion is 'therefore: we don't know, can't know, don't really know that such and such.' E.g.:

> (i) What you perceive are your own sensations; (ii) you never perceive what, if anything, corresponds to them or causes them; therefore: you don't know there are tables and chairs.

Or, another example:

> (i) The only mind you are acquainted with is your own; (ii) all you know about other people is that their bodies behave in certain ways; therefore: you can never really know that another person feels pain, or is worried.

Now in each case the argument, we have agreed, leads to a false conclusion. We *do* know about tables and chairs and other minds. Bearing in mind Ossie Hanfling's units,[1] try to work out the answer to this question: Given that we know the conclusion of the sceptic's argument is false, what else do we know about his argument?●

PRELIMINARY ANSWER

We know that he has made a mistake somewhere. Can you be specific about where? (We know that the mistake must lie in . . . or . . .)●

ANSWER

We know that the mistake lies either in his premises (at least one of which must be false) or in (a step of) his argument, which must be invalid, or in both.

The matter does not end with our saying to the sceptic, 'You are wrong because . . .' We go on to track down where he has made his mistake or mistakes, hunting for the false premise or the invalid step. The great value of scepticism is that the attempts to track down where the sceptical arguments have gone wrong lead one right to the heart of philosophy, and shed a great deal of light on our ordinary common-sense views. In his book *The Problem of Knowledge* A. J. Ayer discusses various responses to scepticism and uses a very nice metaphor to bring out the differences between resting content with knowing that the sceptic is wrong and, on the other hand, going on to track down where he has made his mistake or mistakes. Going on to track down the mistakes is going on a philosophical journey; resting content with knowing he is wrong, is staying at home and never venturing out.

The metaphor could be developed further. The philosophical journey takes one into some very strange territory; travel, as we say, broadens the mind. And when we get home again, having travelled to foreign parts, home does not look quite the same. We view it in a slightly different way. I'll *try* to give an example of this, but don't worry if you don't get the point. We shall be doing it all much more thoroughly in Unit 15.

What do you say to this question: 'Do we perceive the world as it really is?'

If you said, 'We don't know and can't know what the world is really like; perhaps our senses deceive us constantly', you should consider the ordinary use of the phrase 'perceiving things as they really are' and try to construct an argument along the lines of the earlier ones about 'know' and 'absolutely certain'. You are still gripped by scepticism.

If you said, 'Yes, of course, unless we are wearing distorting spectacles, or are drunk, or have taken LSD, etc.', you should consider the following:

---

[1] The relevant quotation is 'The one thing that can not happen is that the premises are true, *and* the argument valid, and yet the conclusion not true'. Units 2B and 9, page 9.

We know that the things we perceive have lots of properties which we don't perceive. We know, for example, that they are all made up of various elements; we know that some things are magnetic, that some are radioactive, but these properties are not properties we can just sense, the way we can just sense that something is red or tastes sweet. Now suppose that when the Martians come, although they cannot sense colour or taste, they are sensitive to magnetism and radioactivity and the presence of e.g. gold in something. Obviously, they don't perceive the world the way we do. Are we right and they wrong? Or the other way round? Or are we both right?

Perhaps you envisaged this possibility anyhow. Perhaps you knew about bats, or read imaginative science fiction. But I think it is often the case that when people say, 'Yes, of course we perceive the world as it really is' they are assuming that this entails 'We perceive it *the* right way and there's only one right way.' Certainly, before I did philosophy, I assumed that. I was what is called a 'naïve realist'. But now I think of our perception of the world, and the fact that our perception of it is correct, in an entirely different way, as I think about my home in a different way after I have been on a journey. I tracked down many of the mistakes the sceptic had made and discovered that many of his mistakes contained grains of truth, and thus a great deal of light was shed on my common-sense views about perceiving the world.

3 PREPARATION FOR THE NEXT UNIT

When I was discussing Arthur Marwick on the subjective element in history, I singled out, but did not discuss, something which I called 'the moral element'. In this unit I was interested in getting clear about what sort of subjective element Marwick thought was *shared* by history and the other disciplines such as the natural sciences, so I did not discuss the moral element because this was something he said was *not* shared by history and the natural sciences. But in the next unit I am going to be discussing moral questions and, as a preliminary, I want you to start thinking about *two* assumptions concerning moral judgements, value judgements and subjectivity. The assumptions are contained in the following passage (which I have constructed).

> The historian simply cannot avoid making value judgements of a type not encountered in the natural sciences, because the historian must sometimes make moral judgements about the past. We saw the disastrous results when the historian tries to be completely neutral. In fact, the historian cannot avoid using words like 'massacre', 'faction', 'ambitious' and so on, all of which imply some kind of moral judgement. So history necessarily contains an important subjective element (which the natural sciences do not contain).

You do *not*, in order to try this exercise, need to have any clear ideas about the distinctions between moral, value and subjective judgements; nor need you know what the imaginary author of the passage thinks, e.g., 'subjective' means. What we have in this constructed passage is two arguments and I am asking you to spot the implicit premises concerning moral, value and subjective judgements. We can do that in an argument without understanding clearly what a writer means by some of the words in his premises. Now please try to write down the two assumptions.●

DISCUSSION

There are of course more than two assumptions lurking in this passage. The two I am interested in are:

(i) Moral judgements are value judgements.
(ii) Value judgements are subjective (or introduce a subjective element).

I think it is clear that the imaginary author of this passage *is* assuming (i) and (ii). How would you make this clear to someone who couldn't see it? (Lay out the arguments of the passage the same way you did in the exercises on pp. 41–42 of Units 2B and 9. Show where the assumptions fit in as premises that are needed. Once again, this does *not* call for an understanding of the terms 'moral judgement', 'value judgement' or 'subjective judgement', but does call for an understanding of validity in argument. Cf. pp. 8–10 of Units 2B and 9.)●

ANSWER

The two arguments of the passage are:

1   The historian cannot avoid making moral judgements; therefore he cannot avoid making value judgements.
2   He necessarily makes value judgements (= he cannot avoid making value judgements); therefore: history necessarily contains a subjective element.

The first argument is relying on assumption (i) above. The full argument would go: The historian cannot avoid making moral judgements; moral judgements are value judgements; therefore: he cannot avoid making value judgements.

The second argument is relying on assumption (ii) above. The full argument would go: The historian necessarily makes value judgements; value judgements introduce a subjective element; therefore: history necessarily contains a subjective element.

What do you think of these two assumptions? *Moral judgements are value judgements. Value judgements are subjective*. Do you think they are obviously true? Are you quite clear about what (1) value judgements and (2) subjective judgements are? Could you give examples of each?

When I first started doing philosophy I was confident that I was perfectly clear about what both value judgements and subjective judgements were and also sure that both assumptions were true. *Given* that I thought both assumptions were true, what must I have thought about moral judgements? (If I was being consistent.)●

ANSWER

I must have thought that moral judgements were subjective. For if (all) moral judgements are value judgements, and if (all) value judgements are subjective, then it follows that (all) moral judgements are subjective.

Well, I did think that. But as my tutors forced me to think harder and more carefully, as they gave me (and as I invented for myself) more and more examples, my initial confidence became eroded. I was no longer sure that both assumptions were true, and this was in part because I found I *wasn't* perfectly clear about what value judgements and subjective judgements were. Everything was revealed to be much more complicated than I had initially supposed. It was also revealed to be much more interesting. I now look back with amazement on the days when, believing that 'all-moral-judgements-are-subjective', I ignored the rich and complex field of moral reasoning. I now find it one of the most fascinating areas of philosophy.

These are purely autobiographical remarks but I hope your experience will be similar and that, if you are not already interested in the complications, I can interest you in them. The best way to start getting involved is to start thinking of the complications for yourself, and the best way to do *that* is to think up your own examples.

Exercises in preparation for Unit 14

I would like you to prepare for reading the next unit by thinking of as many examples as you can of (1) value judgements and (2) subjective judgements. If you watch television or listen to the wireless, try to note down things from there which you think are, or might be, examples. Look out for examples in the newspaper. If you can, ask people around you what they think value and subjective judgements are. See if you can catch yourself making one – if you have young children, what one says to them is often very revealing. Has your tutor marked any of your judgements in your assignments 'subjective' or 'value judgement'? Have you marked that yourself by any judgements in the units?

As well as collecting examples, try to work out what (if anything) you think the two sorts of judgements *are*. I am going to begin the next unit with a large assortment both of rough definitions and examples; if you make the effort to think of some for yourself then, with any luck, some will overlap with mine and then we can discuss them. I should tell you that the developmental-testing students who *did* do this exercise in preparation for the next unit reported that they were glad they had done so.

Starting the next unit without this exercise would be like reading Arnold Kettle's unit on the *Dream* without reading the play. You can, if you *wish*, be entirely passive in your reception of material, but it's much better if you meet what *I* have to say about value and subjective judgements informed by some impressions of your own.

44

UNIT 14 SUBJECTIVITY AND VALUE JUDGEMENTS

CONTENTS

1 VALUE JUDGEMENTS AND SUBJECTIVE JUDGEMENTS

1.1 INTRODUCTION

At the end of the last unit I asked you to start thinking about value judgements and subjective judgements, and to try to collect some examples of each. I hope you have done this because in a minute I am going to give you a whole page of examples and it will be more interesting for you to go through them if you have some of your own.

I also suggested that you ask people around you what they thought value judgements and subjective judgements were, and try to work out rough definitions for yourself. If you haven't done this, I strongly suggest that before reading on, or looking at the Masking Card, you jot down *at least* one definition of 'value judgement' and one of 'subjective judgement'. Please do that now.●

On the Masking Card there are five rough definitions. Let me emphasize immediately that none of these definitions is supposed to be perfect. Nor is the aim of this half of the unit to find out which of, e.g., the three definitions I give of 'subjective judgements' is the ⌜right⌝ definition. There is no ⌜right⌝ definition of either 'value judgements' or 'subjective judgements', because they are both sprawling concepts.

One aim of this first half of the unit is to illustrate this point – that 'value judgements' and 'subjective judgements' are sprawling concepts – and hence to prove that one should *never* assert flatly, 'All value judgements are subjective judgements' or 'All subjective judgements are value judgements.' *Not* because these are rash generalizations, but because, rash or not, they are empty generalizations until one specifies what one means, on this occasion, by 'value judgement' and 'subjective judgement'. Until this is specified one cannot even begin to assess whether the generalization is true or not. Which examples are to count? We don't know.

Each of the definitions I give has an *initial* plausibility. Each one copes with quite a few of the examples we naturally give of either value judgements or subjective judgements. But none of them copes with (i) all and (ii) only the examples we give. Each one either (i) leaves some examples out or (ii) includes some examples we don't want. The point of exploring which ones it includes and which it leaves out is that this enables us to explore different *aspects* of judgements we say are evaluative (= value) or subjective. But, I repeat, there is no one aspect which is the ⌜right⌝ one.

Now I am going to give you my collection of examples. Do *not* puzzle over the way they are grouped. Some are in batches which I refer back to in this unit, but mostly they are my own free association and could be regrouped in dozens of ways. Watch out for your own examples, or ones of mine that you think are like any of yours. *If* you think you know what ⌜the right definition⌝ of either value judgements or subjective judgements is, try it out now.

Jesus was a good man. Hitler was a bad man. *A Midsummer Night's Dream* is a good play. Shakespeare is a good playwright. Hoffman wrote bad musical appreciation. 'The Moon' is a bad poem. Murder is wrong. It's wrong to pick flowers from public parks. It's right to, you ought to, you should, think of others.

There was a massacre, a riot, a rebellion, an uprising. He was a tyrant, a benevolent dictator, an absolute ruler, a patriot, a terrorist, a liberator, an effective ruler. That metaphor is effective, vivid, successful. The rebellion was successful. A faction arose. A101 is boring, interesting, difficult, easy. Doing nothing is boring. Tom Stoppard is amusing. 'I am very proud, revengeful, ambitious,' (Hamlet said).

47

The meal was good value for money. He is in bad health. Smoking is bad for you. That tree has good roots. That dog has good eyesight. That person is a good ruler, a good rider, a good cook, a good chessplayer, a good gardener. He has green fingers. Four is right, five is wrong (as an answer to 'What's twice two?'). If you want to catch the 4.45, you ought to leave now. We should be wary of generalizing hastily. These are good examples of ordinary judgements.

He's a good man, but I wouldn't want him for a friend. He's dishonest but I'm very fond of him. It's her best novel but I don't like it. This is her worst and my favourite. A good pen is no good to me – I'm left-handed.

They live in a slum. They live in a mansion. They have ideas above their station. He's quite irresponsible. He's mad. They had a child and got married. They got married and had a child.

Michael is hungry (said to the people who have eaten all the food, leaving none for Michael). It's sunny again (said by a farmer during a long drought). It's raining! (Same context.) This child's arm is *broken* (said by a doctor to the parent who hasn't noticed). It's food (in the tone that implies 'So eat it and be grateful'). It's hot and wet (said of badly made tea or coffee). It's full of tourists, Americans, students (said in answer to the question 'Why don't you want to go to such and such a place?').

Figure 1 Oliver wants more *food! (said by the person who thinks that Oliver has already had more than he deserves). Engraving by Cruikshank*

He's a kike, a dago, a wop, a nigger, a negro, a commie, a pommie, a pinko.

I love philosophy. I like bananas. I love John. I hate Mary. It's boring. It bores me. It's interesting. It interests me. It's amusing. It amused me. It's difficult. It's difficult for me. It's easy. I find it easy. It's intoxicating. It intoxicates me (makes me drunk). It's poisonous. It would poison me. It's a soporific. It sends me to sleep. It's fatal. It would kill me.

1.2 VALUE JUDGEMENTS

I hope you found the examples interesting. Now we are going on to the definitions. I'm going to imagine that someone called 'A' puts forward the first definition and that someone called 'B' finds fault with it. Once the dialogue has started, *please cover up the rest of the page with your Masking Card* and read on line by line. Now and then I'll ask you to try to anticipate what B could say next. You will be forewarned by the big dot ●. *Don't* assume that if you haven't guessed ⌐right¬, you are wrong. You may well have thought of another good argument for B that I haven't thought of, or which will come up later. Dialogue begins next line.

A: A value judgement is a judgement in which at least one *value* word occurs. [Try to guess the first objection B will make. Then read on.]●

B: That is not much help as a definition unless you tell me what a value word is.

A: A value word is a word such as 'good', 'bad', 'right', 'wrong', etc. You know. The list most philosophers give.

B: Well, I know that is what many philosophers say, but I think they are relying too heavily on that 'etc.' As soon as I try to continue the list I get lost. Do I include, for example, 'faction', 'massacre', 'riot', 'rebellion', 'tyrant'? I'm just not sure.

A: Oh yes, I think you should include most of those. After all, anyone who used them would be making a value judgement. You call someone a tyrant if you are against him; if you are in favour of him you call him a benevolent dictator, and so on. [B will now make *two* objections, one about the 'and so on' and a second about A's use of 'value judgement'. Try to guess, then read on.]●

B: I think you are relying on that 'and so on' the way the other philosophers we mentioned rely on 'etc.' It sounds plausible until I try more examples and then I get lost again. If I say that something is amusing must I be in favour of it? Surely it depends on what it is. I might be against an amusing philosophy assignment – ('Doesn't this person realize that philosophy is a serious subject?') – or an amusing obituary. I might be a Wild Western settler and in favour of massacring Indians though against massacring settlers – you can't tell just from my use of 'massacre', can you?

A: Well . . .

B: Besides, I don't know why we are bothering about value *words*. Originally we wanted to know what they were in order to understand the first definition of value judgements. But you have just introduced the *second* definition on the card, haven't you, with your talk about being for and against? If you haven't, we really have gone round in a complete circle.

A: Yes, I suppose I have. Still, it doesn't matter very much because the two definitions really amount to the same thing. The value words are what we might call 'give-away' words – they give away what the preferences, likes or dislikes of the person who uses them are.

B: 'Good' and 'bad', 'right' and 'wrong' are give-away words?

A: Oh yes, the best examples.

B: You mean whenever anyone uses 'good' or 'better' or 'best' or 'right', he gives away the fact that he likes or prefers or is *for* the thing in question? And whenever he uses 'bad' or 'worst' or 'wrong', he gives away the fact that he *dis*likes, or would choose anything but, or is *against* the things in question?

A: That's right.

B: When*ever*?

A: Oh yes. Unless perhaps he was using the word in a funny way. [B is going to maintain that we can use these words in a perfectly ordinary way without giving away our likes or dislikes. Which examples will he appeal to? Look back to page 48.]●

B: Look at that batch of examples beginning 'The meal was good value for money.' Can you honestly maintain that when*ever* anyone said any of those things, you could tell, from his saying it, that he liked, preferred or was for (or *dis*liked, etc.) the thing in question? I don't give anything away when I say, e.g., 'The meal was good value for money.' What you think I give away is something that you, perfectly reasonably, *assume,* namely that I prefer meals to be good value for money. Of course I'm not denying that by and large we *do* prefer meals to be good value for money, and are (vaguely) against people being in bad health and so on, but not when the meals are offered by a rival restaurant, or the person in bad health is our enemy or a tyrant. That the words themselves don't give away one's preferences is shown by the next lot of examples, where the speaker, speaking quite naturally, cancels the assumption his hearer might have easily made.

A: But if I say that, for instance, such and such is a good poem, don't I imply that I like it?

B: Not automatically. I think that would depend on how skilled you were at literary criticism. For instance, in Units 6–8 you will find the authors discussing a poem called 'If'. They don't actually say they think it is a good poem, but this is in part because they think (and I quote) *'good* and *bad* . . . [are] . . . too emphatic, too bossy'.[1] But I would have found it quite natural if they had said the poem was a good one; they mention lots of good qualities it has. But they don't *like* it and they say so, and they say why. And I would have thought that sort of detachment was perfectly possible. One can appreciate the fact that a poem or a novel or a play is good, or excellent, or even perfect and yet, perhaps for some quite private personal reason, not like it.

A: But suppose we asked someone what his favourite play was and he said, 'I think *A Midsummer Night's Dream* is a *perfect* play!' in an enthusiastic voice? Surely we would know then that he had made a value judgement? [B's response?]●

B: Surely. But *not* just because he used the word 'perfect' (which I suppose you want to say is the value word). We'd know from the context, that is, in this case, his answering the question 'Which do you like most?' and we'd know from the sound of his voice. And once you bring in context or sound of voice, a great variety of judgements count as value judgements, that is, as ones in which the speaker indicates, expresses, conveys, implies, suggests, or gives away what his values are. For instance, 'He's an Open University student.'

A: How could that count as a value judgement? [Can you imagine it said in different ways?]●

B: Well, according to the context and the way it was said it could quite unmistakably convey friendliness ('He's one of us'), scorn ('He's one of *that* lot'), condescension ('Oh, *that* place'), admiration, approval and so on. Here's another example: once you bring in context, you would have to count 'The

[1] Units 6–8, page 147.

desire to find social-economic explanations continues to our day unabated' as a value judgement.

A: Oh, surely not.

B: I think so. It is just that sentence of which Arthur Marwick says, quite correctly, that *in context* it *suggests* that Professor Dickens (i.e. the speaker) is strongly hostile to anything resembling Marxist explanations. It might well include even 'The train for Edinburgh leaves at 10 a.m.'

A: That I do *not* believe – a more neutral remark it would be hard to find.

B: But put it in context. In Units 6–8 they put it in the context of an argument between two people each utterly convinced of his superior knowledge of the facts, and point out that it could convey exasperation, annoyance or scorn. Or suppose that the question is 'What's wrong with going to England by train?' and the answer, in tones of despair, is 'The train for London leaves at 5 a.m.!' And look at those examples beginning 'Michael is hungry'.[1] [End of dialogue. Read on in normal way.]

Given a suitable context, a suitable tone of voice, suitable grounds for the judgement, a vast variety of judgements could, *on* the occasion on which they were made, count as value judgements. A sentence which is a value judgement when made by *one* person on *one* occasion, might not be a value judgement when made by another person on another occasion. To recognize a judgement as a value judgement we need to do more than recognize the words in it; we need to know to what use those words are being put by the speaker.

I am now going to ask you a couple of questions to test your understanding of the preceding few pages. My own specimen answers to them will, in effect, summarize what has been said so far; if you can make yours do the same you will have written a summary of this section. Here is the first question.

What (according to me – you may not agree) is wrong with trying to capture the second sense of 'value judgement' by defining value judgements in terms of value words? I have argued that two things are wrong with that approach. What are they?●

SPECIMEN ANSWER

(i) The first thing wrong with trying to define value judgements in terms of value words is that the definition is circular. We cannot give an independent specification of what a value word is; when we try to say what they are, we simply appeal to the second sense of 'value judgement'. Moreover, (ii) the whole idea of trying to limit value judgements to judgements made in certain words is wrong, because sentences can be value judgements when made by one person on one occasion and not be value judgements when made by another person on another occasion. Here is the second question.

Can you think of an example of a judgement which you wouldn't expect to be a value-judgement ordinarily, and describe a context in which it *would* be a value judgement?●

Sentences such as those in the batch beginning 'Michael is hungry' illustrate the point that sentences you wouldn't ordinarily think of as being value judgements can be value judgements in a certain context (in certain circumstances), said in a certain tone of voice.

---

[1] Further discussion of such examples, and others, related to the problem of meaning in context, can be heard in the interdisciplinary philosophy and literature radio programme, 'Fact and Value' (Radio Programme 15).

Now I am going to ask you a question which looks forward to the next section. Remember that one aim of this unit is to encourage you to think critically and patiently about such sweeping vague generalizations as 'All moral judgements are value judgements' or 'All value judgements are subjective judgements.' One definition of 'subjective judgement' which Arthur Marwick quoted was 'not strictly in accordance with the facts', and it is one of the possible definitions I have put on the Masking Card. Although we haven't discussed 'subjective' yet, we have just been doing 'value judgement'. So now consider this question: Are all value judgements subjective in the sense of not being strictly in accordance with the facts? (Look back at the examples used in answer to the second question above)●

SPECIMEN ANSWER

No. Perhaps some, perhaps even quite a lot of value judgements are not strictly in accordance with the facts; the discussion so far does not show whether this is so or not. But it certainly shows that not *all* value judgements are not strictly in accordance with the facts. The examples in the batch beginning 'Michael is hungry' can all be put in contexts in which they are *both* value judgements *and* strictly in accordance with the facts. So *not* all value judgements are subjective according to this definition of 'subjective'.

Now we shall go on to another possible definition.

1.3   SUBJECTIVE JUDGEMENTS

The second definition

Let's look at the second definition of 'subjective judgement' on the Masking Card. How do we spot whether a judgement is subjective in this sense, that is, made *because* the speaker is biased, prejudiced or influenced by personal feelings? Well, it might contain another sort of give-away word, that is, a word which gives away the fact that its user is biased or prejudiced, because it is a word which *by and large* only people who are biased or prejudiced use. We have to remember the 'by and large'. Blacks who describe themselves or each other as niggers may hold their own race in contempt, but you couldn't infer their attitude solely from their use of the word. Or a child using such a word may not know it is offensive and use it in all innocence, without realizing that there is a more respectful alternative. What is offensive may vary. John Ferguson told me that when he was in Nigeria in 1966 'Negro' was innocent and 'Black' was offensive; but that when he went to America it was the other way around. What is offensive varies from country to country, from generation to generation, perhaps even from street to street. So identifying a word as a give-away word is not a perfectly simple matter.

But things become even more difficult when we move away from judgements containing give-away words. Consider the following little dialogues:

A child asks, 'Why can Jane have a baby and John not have a baby?' and the answer the child is given is 'Because Jane's a woman and John's a man. Women can have babies and men can't.'

The child asks, 'Why did Jane fail the logic exam. and John pass it?' The answer the child is given is 'Because Jane's a woman and John's a man. Women can't think logically and men can.'

We shall now have another dialogue between A and B. A is going to say that the second answer is bad because it is subjective. As before, cover up the rest of the page with your card and read on line by line.

A: The answer to the child's second question is bad because it's subjective. It's a biased and prejudiced answer.

B: You mean the *words* are biased and prejudiced?

A: Yes. [At this point try to anticipate what B could say next. Then read on.]●

B: But *words* aren't biased or prejudiced. It's people who are biased or pre-judiced, though of course you can often tell from what they say that they are biased or prejudiced.

A: Yes, of course, that's what I meant. If someone said, 'Jane failed the logic exam. and John didn't because Jane's a woman and John's a man; women can't think logically and men can', you could tell from their words – from their saying that – that they are biased and prejudiced. [Remembering what we have just been discussing, that is, give-away words, what question does B now ask? Try to guess and then read on.]●

B: How could you tell? None of the words are what we called give-away words.

A: I agree. This time it's not a matter of the particular words used. But it's the sort of answer which only biased or prejudiced people would give.

B: I'm not sure what you mean by 'the sort of answer'. What is there about it which makes it the sort of answer which only biased or prejudiced people would give?

A: It draws a distinction between the capacities of men and women. It's only sexually prejudiced people who do that. [Try to guess what B will say in objection to this.]●

B: But the first answer drew a distinction between the capacities of men and women. It said that women can have babies and men can't. And surely there's nothing wrong with *that* answer; you can't say that only sexually prejudiced people would say *that*. [Now try something on A's behalf. What might he try next?]●

Figure 2 She: *Why do people say you can think logically and I can't?*
He: *I can't conceive*

A: I didn't make myself quite clear. Of course there's nothing wrong with the first answer. But the difference between the first and the second answer is that the first draws a *true* distinction between the capacities of men and women, whereas the second draws a *false* one. It's just not true that *no* women can think logically and *all* men can, which is what the answer supposes. It's because it draws a false distinction that you can tell that the answer is given by a biased or prejudiced person. [There is an implicit assumption in that last sentence of A's which B is now going to make explicit. Can you see what it is?]●

B: You mean it's only biased or prejudiced people who believe or say things that are false?

A: Uhmm. Well, I can't say that. I admit that the most unbiased, unprejudiced, rational, fair-minded people still make mistakes and believe what is false.

B: So it's *not* simply because the answer draws a false distinction that you can tell that it is given by a biased or prejudiced person.

A: All right; I admit there's more to it than that the answer involves a mistake. There's also the question of the *sort* of mistake it is. No-one could make that sort of mistake unless they were biased or prejudiced. *No-one.* [What will B say now?]●

B: I'm going to give a counter-example. [If you have already thought of a counter-example, read on. If you have not, try to think of one now.]●
Imagine that the *answers* are given by a child, and that in the second case the child goes on, 'because there's a little bit in your brain that can do logic and the bit that women have makes babies instead'. Surely the child is not biased or prejudiced, but simply wrong. He doesn't know the facts. [Your counter-example need not have been one involving a child. Any example of someone believing in the distinction out of innocence or ignorance, or through having been misinformed, would have done.]●

A: I agree that I overstated my case. I should have remembered the importance of context. Of course *in practice* it is often absolutely certain that the person who gives something like the second answer is biased or prejudiced, and I forgot that *in practice* we usually know about the context. We know whether the person is a grown-up or a child; we know if we are speaking to them that they live in the twentieth century; if we are reading what they said we usually know what period they were writing in. Forgetting this made me overlook something very important – [what do you think it is?]●
– namely, what sorts of *grounds* the person has for his judgement. A person can have good grounds for a judgement which, despite being good grounds, consist of falsehoods. In *practice* we often know straight off whether a person has made a false judgement because he has good, though false, grounds for it, or whether he has made it without good grounds, because he is biased or prejudiced. In *theory* we can't tell from the falsity of the judgement that it is subjective, that is, made because the person is biased or prejudiced. In theory, we always have to ask about the grounds. [So what has A learned by now – thinking of where the dialogue began?]●

A: So, going back to where we started, I must admit that I have learned something rather important, and that is, never to call a judgement subjective in this sense until I know what the speaker's grounds were for saying what he said. He might even be biased and prejudiced about the matter, but he might not have made the judgement *because* he was biased or prejudiced.

B: Good. Let me ask one more question. We have just agreed that I can know a judgement is false, and still *not* know whether it is subjective, that is, made because the person is biased or prejudiced. I have to know whether the person who made it had good grounds for what he said. Well, if I know a judgement is *true,* then do I know, straight off, that it's *not* subjective, that is, *not* made because the person was biased or prejudiced, or, once again, do I have to know whether the person who made it had good grounds for what he said? [Can you answer this question? Think of an example or an argument to support your answer. You can then uncover the text and read on as usual, not line by line.]●

The answer to B's question is that no, I don't know straight off that a true judgement is not subjective. Yes, once again, I have to know whether the person who made it had good grounds for what he said. Think back to the witnesses in court in the last unit. Suppose we have got to the point where it is proven that the accused did the murder: this has become clear from the evidence of various witnesses. But then we get another witness who says, 'I *know* the accused did the murder, I'm absolutely certain, because he's a beastly horrible man and I hate him; he's always shouting at my children when they play outside his house; he must be utterly heartless.'

This person's judgement that the accused did the murder is (according to the way I have set up the example) *true*; but unless he has better grounds for the judgement than those he has given, the judgement is clearly subjective – he makes it *because* he is biased, prejudiced and influenced by personal feelings.

If you thought of an example of your own, make sure that it has all three of the relevant characteristics, that is, make sure it is an example of (i) a *true* judgement which someone makes (ii) *not* on the basis of good grounds but (iii) *because* he is biased, prejudiced or influenced by personal feelings.

If you couldn't think of an example (some people find it much easier than others), you can still argue for your answer by pointing to the simple fact that a person could come, by bias or prejudice, under the influence of personal feelings, to believe something which was true *and* for which there was excellent evidence, without knowing about the evidence. It might be very rare; in practice it might not be something we have to worry about much. But in theory it could happen, so in theory we can *not* tell from the truth of a judgement that it is not subjective.

Summary of this section

Answer the following in complete and informative sentences and the summary will write itself.

1   What is it that (usually) shows bias, prejudice or the influence of personal feelings in a speaker – his judgement itself or the grounds he has for it?
2   What are the rare (and not easily identified) exceptions?
3   Can you tell from a judgement's being false that it is subjective?
4   Can you tell from its being true that it is not subjective?●

MY SUMMARY

(1) Bias, prejudice or the influence of personal feelings is mostly shown by the grounds the speaker has for his judgement, not by the judgement itself. (2) Unless the judgement contains a give-away word (and these are not always easily identified), you cannot tell from the judgement alone that the person who made it did so *because* he was biased, prejudiced or influenced by personal feelings. (3) You can't tell from the judgement's being false that it was made because the speaker was biased, etc. (rather than because he was ignorant or misled). And (4) you can't tell from its being true that it wasn't made because the speaker was prejudiced, biased, etc. In either case you have to know the grounds.

Here a new thought can come up. What if I have *no* grounds for a judgement; it is not that I have bad ones: I just don't have any at all? *Must* my judgement then be subjective, that is, made *because* I am biased or prejudiced or influenced by personal feelings?

I think not. For one thing, some judgements don't even seem to call for grounds. 'I don't like the taste of this cheese', 'I find the rhythm brisk, chirpy, almost cheerful' – if we made such remarks and someone said, 'What are your grounds?' we wouldn't know what to say. There are others which we do not think of trying to give grounds for until the sceptic upsets us. I say I saw Bill yesterday; those *are* my grounds for claiming he was in town yesterday; no-one thinks to ask me what my grounds are for saying that I saw Bill yesterday. I say I can see the milk on the table, and those *are* my grounds for saying that it *is* on the table and not in the refrigerator; no-one thinks to ask me what my grounds are for saying I can see the milk.

When the sceptic challenges me I can try to rationalize my judgements and manufacture grounds. But this would not be very honest; nor would it be wise, for whatever I produce he will challenge and where will the giving of grounds for grounds for grounds end?[1]

Why do I not come straight out and say I have no grounds? No-one, not even the sceptic, will come forward and say that it is quite likely that I am *mistaken* and am letting bias, prejudice or personal feelings blind me to the truth. And saying I have no grounds only sounds disreputable when it was expected that I had them. But no-one, including the sceptic, *expects* me to have grounds for such judgements. So I think it is all right to come straight out and say that, for certain judgements, one has no grounds, *but* that this does not entail that the judgements are subjective in the sense that one makes them *because* one is biased, prejudiced, or influenced by personal feelings.

Comprehension question on this section

If a judgement is subjective in the sense that the person who made it, made it because he was biased, prejudiced or influenced by personal feelings, is it also subjective in the sense that it is not strictly in accordance with the facts? Please write your answer down. This *is* a comprehension question on what has gone before – if you are not certain of your answer, or if your answer does not seem to you to connect with the preceding discussion, I suggest you look back at page 55.●

SPECIMEN ANSWER

It might be or it might not be. As we saw in the example of the murder witness, it is possible to have a judgement which is straightforwardly true, that is, strictly in accordance with the facts, but which is made by someone because he is (in this case) influenced by personal feelings. Whether a judgement is in accordance with the facts or otherwise is a separate issue from that of whether the person who made it did so because he was biased or prejudiced or influenced by feelings.

So, not all judgements which are subjective in the sense of the second definition are subjective in the sense of the first definition.

Finally, a question to tie this section to the preceding one. I have defined a value judgement as one in which the speaker indicates, expresses, conveys, etc. what his preferences, likes or dislikes are. That would surely cover indicating (expressing, conveying, etc.) his biases, prejudices and personal feelings. So aren't all value judgements, thus defined, subjective in the sense that they are made because the speaker is biased, prejudiced, influenced by personal feelings? Please write your answer down.●

SPECIMEN ANSWER

Not necessarily. We should never call a judgement subjective in this sense until we knew what the speaker's grounds were for saying what he did. He might

---

[1] Cf. Radio Programme 14, associated with this unit, and the programme notes.

even be biased or prejudiced, or have strong feelings about the matter, but still not have made the judgement *because* he was biased or prejudiced or had been influenced by those feelings.

This is an important point, because overlooking it often leads one to overlook good arguments and do people grave injustices. I notice amongst some of my Women's Lib. friends a tendency not to bother to listen to the grounds people have for judgements indicating male chauvinism. They slide from 'His saying that clearly indicates he is a male chauvinist' to 'Therefore he believes it *because* he is a male chauvinist' and thence to 'Therefore he does not have good grounds, he makes that judgement *because* he is prejudiced.' Other common examples are found in political and religious discussions. 'He's only saying that because he's a Tory', 'Well, of course he says that – what else would you expect a Marxist to say', 'Naturally he says abortion is wrong – he's a Catholic.' Or, to go back to an earlier example, 'These Western scientific blokes are all against Uri Geller – typical prejudice.' But the Tory, the Marxist, the Catholic and the scientist, though they might have spoken out of prejudice or bias, influenced by their personal feelings, might, rather, have good grounds for what they say on *this* matter, which one would benefit from learning about.

1.4 SUBJECTIVE JUDGEMENTS

The third definition

Let's go on to the last definition of 'subjective judgement' on the card. This may have struck you as an odd one. It is odd, though almost straight out of the *Shorter Oxford Dictionary;* it relates to an old use of 'subjective', according to which it means 'relating to a thinking *subject*', and is obviously related to one sense of 'subjective judgement' we used in the last unit, namely a judgement in which there is some *personal* involvement. I found I needed it in part to get clear about a muddle, or ambiguity, in the second definition, namely the bit about 'influenced by personal feelings'.

I think there is an obvious difference between the following two cases.

Case I: I say, 'John did the murder' and I say it *because* I hate John like poison and find it only too easy to believe, on the rather circumstantial evidence available, that he did it.
Case II: I say, 'I hate John' and I say it because I do hate John.

These are both cases in which the judgement was made because the speaker was influenced by personal feelings; hence, according to the second definition, they are both subjective. But we don't think of cases like the second one when we are talking about subjective judgements in the bias/prejudice/feelings sense. At least one reason (probably not the only reason) for this is that we think judgements shouldn't be made *because* one is biased, prejudiced or influenced by feelings: this is not a rational way to make them. This is true – except when the judgements are *about* one's personal feelings. Then it would be irrational *not* to be influenced by them.

When we consider judgements *about* (and hence influenced by) the speaker's personal feelings, or reactions, we start finding lots of new examples. Some of mine are in the batch on page 49 beginning 'I love philosophy.' A and B are now going to discuss this batch. Cover up the text as usual.

B: I must say I think Rosalind has made a mistake in putting all those examples together. I would have said they fall into two quite distinct groups. [Can you guess which the two groups are?]●
There are all the ones which really are about the speaker, the ones containing 'I' or 'me'; and then there's the other group which is impersonal and doesn't contain any personal pronouns.

A: Surely that is a purely grammatical distinction. [What will A say to support this – something about meaning?]•

All the judgements are personal reaction judgements – 'It is boring, fascinating, amusing, entertaining, moving, etc.' mean just the same as 'It bores, fascinates, amuses, etc. *me*' or 'Personally I find it boring, fascinating, amusing, etc.' None of them are judgements about 'it' – whatever it is. They are all judgements or remarks about the speaker. The speaker is the *subject* of the remark, hence 'subjective'.

B: I don't think the impersonal ones mean exactly the same as the others. If they do then why – [why what?]•

– is it sometimes appropriate to use one and sometimes the other? Just stylistic grounds?

A: Mmmm, you're right. There's more to it than that. [When do you think the impersonal ones are appropriate, and when the personal ones?]•

Perhaps we make the judgement sound impersonal when we expect or would like to think that other people will agree, that is, react the same way as us; and we make it explicitly about ourselves when we expect that our personal reaction is idiosyncratic, unusual, rare – or suspect it might be.

B: Yes, I think something like that is right. And that gives us the distinction between the two groups.

A: All right; have the distinction if you want it. But you will surely agree that they *are* all subjective in this special sense we are discussing, that is, they are all judgements in which the speaker says something about himself, his feelings or reactions. Even if the impersonal ones are about the probable reactions of other people, they are *also* about the speaker's. 'It's boring, but it doesn't bore me' sounds *very* odd.

B: I could quibble about that – 'He's very charming but he doesn't charm me' sounds all right – but it would be more or less a quibble. Let's call them all subjective. What I'm more interested in is whether these subjective judgements are subjective in the first sense, that is, not strictly in accordance with the facts. [What do you think? Don't try to anticipate A or B, just think about it. Then read on as usual].

1.5   SUBJECTIVE JUDGEMENTS

The first definition

One thing is perfectly clear and that is that there is no reason why 'This poem bores me' or 'I find this poem boring' shouldn't be strictly in accordance with the facts. That something bores me, fascinates me, amuses me, etc. are perfectly good facts and the judgements accord with them. But what about '*It* is boring, amusing, fascinating'?

Common sense says: What is the difficulty? That something bores, fascinates or amuses lots of people, or most people (or *would* bore, fascinate or amuse lots of people or most people) are equally good facts, and judgements such as 'It is boring, fascinating, amusing' can be made strictly in accordance with them.

There is also a pull towards saying the following: 'But there *is* a difficulty. That something *is* boring, fascinating or amusing is not an objective fact about the thing. Things bore and fascinate people all right, but not because they *are* boring or fascinating. Things, like fires and the sun, heat people because they *are* hot. Being hot is a real objective property they have. But things aren't *really* boring, fascinating, etc. We can only talk as though they were because there is some measure of agreement in personal reactions, i.e. we are bored, fascinated, etc.'

1.6 AGREEMENT IN REACTION

There are two possible responses to this view that there is a difficulty. One is philosophically very sophisticated and if you even half thought of it, that is very good. It is to argue that agreement in reaction is required for talk about all sorts of things, perhaps even for talk about anything at all. One could begin by mentioning a few of the examples I gave in the batch that followed the ones we have just been discussing. A few things are poisonous to only a few people and then we say so explicitly, but mostly we do not need to. Since there is a large measure of agreement in physical reaction, we can talk about things being poisonous full stop. In the next unit we shall see that it can be argued that things are not ⌐really⌐ coloured, since we can only talk about things being, for example, red or white, because of agreement in reaction.

The argument can be extended beyond these few examples. Do you remember that in the previous unit I pointed out that Ossie Hanfling was assuming in his units that by and large we were going to agree whether a conclusion had been supported or not? And I had said that if we didn't agree with him and each other most of the time we wouldn't be able to talk about ordinary justification or the supporting of conclusions at all. So, in a way, we can only talk about things being justified or supported, proved or known, because of agreement in reaction.

If you find all this mind-boggling, or are beginning to say, 'So *everything* is subjective', don't think about it any more. Just go straight on to the next paragraph and *forget* it.

The other possible response is to say: Well, since there *is* some measure of agreement in reaction, what is wrong with relying on it? Saying that these judgements are subjective (because not strictly in accordance with the facts, because there aren't ⌐really⌐ objective facts for them to be in accordance with) makes them *sound* disreputable. They are made to sound like judgements we shouldn't make; judgements that shouldn't be printed in Open University units, or written in assignments. But it turns out that the only crime we are committing in making such judgements is the ⌐crime⌐ of presupposing what is, in fact, the case!

When you read, or re-read, other units in this course, in particular the literature and music units, you might watch out for the many occasions on which the writers assume agreement in reaction – and note how completely plausible their assumptions seem to be.

I am now going to put some of these distinctions to work. The following is a paraphrase of someone writing a piece of literary criticism.

> 'When, like a running grave, time tracks you down' is a vivid and effective metaphor, better than Cowper's 'My fugitive years are all hasting away.' 'Running grave' appeals directly to the sense of sight, we see something running, whereas in Cowper's line 'fugitive' and 'hasting' only *dimly* suggest movement. The line expresses fear of death and the idea is intimately connected with the feeling conveyed by the metaphor. We cannot see a grave running, so the very vagueness carries menace, and while the running movement is menacing because unidentifiable, it is also made more fearsome by the connection with 'grave'.

In what senses, if any, could this passage be said to be subjective? Well, the writer's judgement that the metaphor is vivid and effective is apparently *not* made *because* he is biased, prejudiced or influenced by personal feelings; on the contrary, he gives good grounds for saying it is vivid and effective. So not subjective according to the second definition. The passage is, minimally, about the writer, in that it at least strongly suggests that *he* finds the metaphor vivid and effective, and it is both explicitly and implicitly about him and us. *We* cannot see a grave running; the very vagueness carries menace (to *us*) . . . it is made more fearsome (to *us*) by the connection with 'grave'. So the passage is subjective in the third sense. As for whether it is in accordance with the facts: well, it certainly *is* a fact that many people find the unknown menacing, and most of us fear death to some extent. Is the judgement that the metaphor is vivid and effective in accordance with the facts? Obviously it might not work for a race of creatures who actually welcomed the thought of dying; nor to a race of creatures who could neither see nor hear things running. It would only work for people with, and capable of, certain reactions. But it works for us; as far as we are concerned, it is a fact that the metaphor is vivid and effective. So the passage is *not* subjective in the sense of not being strictly in accordance with the facts.

1.7 CONCLUSION OF THIS PART OF THE UNIT

One non-constructive way to react to such passages is to hit on the word 'better' in the first sentence and say, 'Oh well, "better" is a value-word, *so* that's a value judgement, *so* it's subjective, *so* it's a personal remark, *so* it's not a matter of fact, *so* I needn't bother to think seriously or critically about anything he says about it.' To react in this way is to prejudge the issue of proof in the arts which I mentioned in the introduction to the previous unit.

I maintained that the imaginary writer of the passage gave good grounds for saying that the metaphor is vivid and effective; he also says something in support of the judgement that Cowper's metaphor is *not* vivid and effective, and these together give good grounds for saying the first metaphor is better than Cowper's. If one thinks that Cowper's is at least *as* vivid and effective (and that neither is better than the other), then this is a judgement for which one should try to give grounds, comparable in detail *and plausibility* to those given in support of the running grave. If one thinks the first metaphor is *not* vivid and effective then one should try to make clear why it fails *despite* the points the writer makes which are so obviously in its favour. Saying, 'Well, it doesn't work for me' is, so far, nothing but a piece of gratuitous psychological autobiography. If it doesn't work for me I should try to work out whether this is a particularly personal idiosyncratic reaction on my part, or whether I'm reacting as I would expect many other people to react, because I would expect them to agree with me that . . . and in there go some grounds for saying the metaphor is a failure, or a bad one, or not as good as Cowper's.

What I hope to have achieved in this part of the unit is to have persuaded you that you should *never* say, 'Snap! That's a value judgement. Snap! That's subjective' without going on to say, 'That is, it contains a value word or it indicates that the speaker is in favour of or . . .' You certainly *don't* have to go on to give one of my definitions. I hope you found them useful in sorting out different aspects of judgements we say are evaluative or subjective but perhaps you will now find it more useful to discard them and think of others for yourself. But remember, if you do try to do that, you are not trying to find *the perfect* definition. There is no simple answer to the question 'But what *is* a value judgement, *really*?' A value judgement is, really, what I gave in the first definition, *or* the second, *or* in other definitions I thought of but didn't have room for, *or* what would be given in other definitions that you or other people might think of. The same goes for 'What is subjectivity *really*?' It is all the things I have said it is, and several more besides.

What will you now do if someone asks you whether (all) value judgements are subjective?

If someone asks us, 'Have you stopped beating your wife yet?' or 'Are you as big a fool as you look?' we can all spot that those questions presuppose something that most of us at least want to reject. I hope you will by now agree with me that 'Are value judgements subjective – yes or no?' presupposes something that should be rejected, namely that the terms involved are clear-cut and unambiguous and hence that a simple yes/no answer can be given. And I hope that by now you would, if asked that question, *pounce* on that presupposition and question it. Thus joining the ranks of philosophers who have infuriated their friends by saying, 'Well, it all depends on what you mean by . . .'

2 UTILITARIANISM

2.1 INTRODUCTION

The first half of this unit has been about value judgements and subjective judgements. This half is about moral judgements, but I am not going to discuss them in the same way as I discussed the others. Instead of discussing moral judgements in general – what count as examples and what do not, different aspects of judgements we say are moral, and so on – instead of doing that, I'm going to discuss the moral judgements involved in the moral doctrine called 'utilitarianism'.

One definition of utilitarianism which may be given is this: Utilitarianism is the doctrine according to which actions are made right or wrong by their good or bad consequences. A more familiar definition would be this: Utilitarianism is the doctrine according to which actions are right in so far as they promote happiness, wrong in so far as they produce the reverse of happiness.

The reason I mention the first definition is that it makes *very* plain something which the second definition tends to conceal, namely that utilitarianism is what is called a *consequentialist* doctrine. According to (most forms of) utilitarianism, actions are not themselves intrinsically right or wrong; they are right or wrong in so far as they have good or bad *consequences*. (You will see the significance of this when we get on to the examples below.)

In the more familiar definition, the good consequences are identified explicitly. The version of utilitarianism which holds that they consist in the greatest happiness of the greatest number was popularized by Jeremy Bentham and his

Figure 3   Jeremy Bentham (1748–1831), painted by Pickersgill

Figure 4   John Stuart Mill (1806–1873)

disciple John Stuart Mill and from them we have the terms 'Greatest Happiness Principle' (sometimes abbreviated to 'GHP') and 'Principle of Utility' (hence 'Utilitarianism'). This is the version I shall be discussing, so from now on whenever I say 'utilitarianism' I mean 'Bentham and Mill's version of utilitarianism'. (But remember that it is consequentialist.)

Utilitarianism is an attractive doctrine (1) because it gives simple straightforward answers to what seem to be simple, straightforward questions and (2) because the answers appear, on the face of it, to be right. Let me now elaborate on those two points.

2.2   SIMPLE ANSWERS

Suppose I ask the general questions, 'How ought I to regulate my conduct?' or 'What should be my guiding principle in life?' These seem to be quite straightforward questions. They might, of course, be very difficult to answer correctly, but they do not look as though they want more than one-sentence answers. And utilitarianism gives them a one-sentence answer: 'Always act in accordance with the greatest happiness principle.'

Many other ethical doctrines have attempted to produce one-sentence answers to those questions, e.g. 'Love and do what you will', 'So act, that the rule on which thou actest would admit of being adopted as a law by all rational beings', 'Follow the dictates of your conscience', 'Obey the ten commandments' and so on.

But these one-sentence answers have a tendency to prove insufficiently specific when applied to a particular occasion. On a particular occasion, faced with a moral dilemma, I ask myself the question, 'What should I do in *these* circumstances?' and the one-sentence answers often either do not make it clear what I should do, or, even worse, yield conflicting answers. What should I do when the person I love is dying slowly in agony? It is precisely because I love them that I both value their life and want to end their suffering, so 'Love and do what you will' yields conflicting answers. So does my conscience, which tells me both to respect their right to life and to spare them suffering. The rule 'Respect life' *and* the rule 'End suffering' both seem to be rules which could be acted on by all rational beings – so which one should I act on on *this* occasion? The ten commandments are perfectly clear on this issue – 'Thou shalt not kill' and that is that. But what should I do when my choice lies between killing one or letting many die? (When, for example, I can only stop the madman from throwing the bomb into the crowd by pushing him backwards to blow himself up.) Am I supposed to interpret 'Thou shalt not kill' in accordance with the cynical little couplet:

> Thou shalt not kill, but needst not strive,
> Officiously, to keep alive.

Utilitarianism cuts straight through these problems and provides a tailor-made answer – tailor-made, apparently, for every possible situation – 'Of the alternative actions possible, do the one which will promote the greatest happiness of the greatest number of people involved, or, where that is not possible, do whatever causes the least suffering to the smallest number'.

2.3   THE ANSWERS APPEAR TO BE RIGHT

The second point I made about utilitarianism was that its answers 'appear, on the face of it, to be right'. Right, that is, in so far as they involve saying that suffering is wrong, that we ought not to make people suffer but ought to aim at preventing suffering, and that the promotion of happiness is right, that we ought to do as we would be done by and aim, where possible, at making everyone as happy as they can be. It is especially plausible in the version that stresses *foreseen* rather than actual consequences; it directs me to do what I foresee will make everyone happy, allowing that the actual consequences may not be as I foresee. Obviously if I intend to produce good consequences and produce bad ones unintentionally, through unforeseeable circumstances, I should not be condemned for doing wrong.

I do not feel at all compelled to put scare quotes around the words 'right' and 'wrong' and 'ought' and 'should' in the above paragraph. And if you dismiss the remarks in the above paragraph as 'value judgements' or 'but that's subjective' then the first part of this unit failed in its aim. Yes, they contain so-called value words – I could hardly discuss ethics without using such words as 'right', 'wrong' and 'ought'. Perhaps they indicate that I am against human suffering and in favour of people being happy, but that is hardly disreputable. Aren't you?

Are my remarks about suffering being wrong and the promotion of happiness right etc. subjective in any of the three senses I gave on the masking card? This is a very big question, which is being hotly debated by moral philosophers at the moment. It is far too big a question to discuss here, and far too important to prejudge. But just suppose that, at the very worst, the remarks were subjective in some way or ways. Would that be so very bad?

We have already seen that judgements which rely on and involve agreement in personal reaction are still worth making and worth reading. What about the question whether I say suffering is wrong and human happiness a good thing because I am biased or prejudiced? Well, you want to know what my grounds are before you can decide that and I hope to disarm you by saying I do not have grounds for saying that either of these judgements is true. They *are* my grounds for many other moral judgements; with them I hit rock bottom. If someone said he thought they were false I would seriously doubt whether I could discuss ethics with him at all.[1]

That we hit rock bottom, in the giving of grounds, somewhere along the line, is not peculiar to ethics, somehow rendering it particularly disreputable. Remember that we hit rock bottom with 'The rhythm is brisk, chirpy, almost cheerful.' And remember how bizarre the philosophical sceptic would appear in court if he said that perhaps the witness's senses were deceiving him, or perhaps he had been dreaming, so perhaps it was false that the witness saw and talked to the accused. How could we discuss what happens in the world with a man who will not accept what he sees and hears as grounds for what is there? How could we discuss the future with a man who will not accept what has happened already as grounds for judgements about what will happen tomorrow? Consider Ossie Hanfling's example: 'All men are mortal, Socrates is a man, therefore Socrates is mortal.' What could we do with someone who denied that that is a valid argument? It just *is* a valid argument; if someone denied it I would seriously doubt whether I could argue with him at all.

Someone might say: But with the probable exception of the rhythm example, no-one does deny those things. But surely ethics, like music and poetry, is culture-relative. When you say that it is wrong to make people suffer and right to make them happy, you are speaking with the biases and prejudices of your own age and culture. Other cultures think differently.

This too needs a lengthy discussion and, barred from that, I shall make two brief remarks. One is that I should like to hear more about these cultures: a culture which believes that suffering ennobles the soul and leads to greater happiness in the next life or the after-life is still possibly a culture with which we share some common ground about right and wrong. After all, we too, though believing that it is wrong to cause suffering, think it is right to send our children to the dentist for the sake of their having good teeth in later life. Perhaps we differ from these people only in our confidence about the after-life and how it can be affected or altered, but not, fundamentally, about right and wrong.[2]

---

[1] That we cannot go on giving grounds, but must stop somewhere, is the topic discussed in Radio Programme 14.

[2] That a surface disagreement about what ought to be done is not sufficient to prove cultural relativism, is one of the two points I hope you will get out of the 'Jumpers' television programme (Television Programme 14). When people appeal to cultural variation to prove the relativity or so-called subjectivity of morals, they are, I suppose, thinking of cultural variation in ethical behaviour as if it were parallel to as simple a thing as variation in taste. We don't like eating rotten shark; to some cultures it is a great delicacy. There is no disagreement between us as to the facts; we and they simply (it is said) attach different values to the fact. They go for rotten shark and we don't. The parallel is supposed to be: We disapprove of cannibalism; some cultures regard it not only as permissible, but as something that ought to be done. There is no disagreement between us as to the facts; we and they simply attach different values to the facts. They go for cannibalism and we don't.

In *Jumpers*, the example George uses is that the people in the other culture go for eating their elders whereas we go for burying them in teak boxes. At first sight this is very like one culture's going for eating rotten shark and the other culture's not. But George's (or Stoppard's) point is that this is *not* just like variation in taste. We and they do *not* agree on the facts, for they believe that they confer honour on their parents by eating them, which we certainly do not. And though we and they do not agree on the facts it seems that in this case we all actually do agree on the so-called values. For both sides agree that *if* such and such is honouring one's parents, then it is something that ought to be done.

The second remark is that it is of course quite possible that we might not be able to discuss ethical questions with all other cultures, just as we might not be able to discuss music and poetry with them. Indeed there might be a culture which did not *have* an ethical system. They would not think *differently* from us about right and wrong: they wouldn't think about right and wrong at all, that is, would not have the concepts.

But I am assuming that, in addressing you, I am addressing someone who, like me, thinks it is wrong to make people suffer and right to make them happy, and would not be clear how to set about arguing with someone who disagreed. I am also going to assume that we agree on certain other examples of right and wrong. It may be that you disagree with some of them; if and when that happens *don't* say to yourself, 'Well, that just shows the pointlessness of arguing about something as ⌈subjective⌉ as morals.' If you say that, you just stop thinking constructively. Instead, try to substitute an example of your own and see if the argument will then flow on.

2.4   PROBLEMS FOR UTILITARIANISM

So the assumption is that we are utilitarians to *some* extent; that the utilitarian greatest happiness principle is at least *one* of our basic moral principles. But are we total utilitarians? Do we regard it as the supreme moral principle? I think it is most helpful to think about that question in terms of three others:

(i) Is everything we think wrong, wrong *because* it violates the greatest-happiness principle?
(ii) Is everything we think right, right *because* it is in accordance with the principle?
(iii) If someone were a genuine utilitarian through and through would they fulfil our ideal of a truly moral person? Do we want our friends to be utilitarians? Do we want to bring our children up to be?

I'm going to begin by discussing (i). Try to think of some counter-examples, i.e. examples of things which are either utterly wrong, but don't come out wrong on utilitarian grounds, or at least arguably wrong, but straightforwardly justifiable and right on utilitarian grounds. When you have, or if you can't, read on and you will find that I have *sketched* counter-examples. If they are not the ones you have thought of (either because you thought of different ones or did not think of any), see if you can work out why I have given them as counter-examples. Remember that utilitarianism is a *consequentialist* doctrine.●

(1) Utilitarianism can't cope with murder. (2) It can justify both a judge's allowing a criminal to go unpunished and (3) his allowing an innocent man to be punished. (4) It justifies an examiner passing someone who has written fail-level papers and assignments. (5) It justifies breaking promises. (6) It justifies a whole range of anti-social activities such as picking flowers from public parks, dropping litter, not paying bus fares, walking on the grass where the notices forbid it, hosing your garden during a water shortage, etc.

Can you see why these might be thought to pose problems for utilitarianism? Let's go through them.

2.4.1   *Murder*

Utilitarianism has two difficulties with murder: (a) in saying what is ever wrong with it and (b), supposing it has solved that problem, in saying why it is wrong in certain cases.

(a) This objection to utilitarianism tends to sound crazy. Murder not wrong according to utilitarianism? When it is the doctrine of humanitarianism! How absurd! But remember that it is a consequentialist doctrine. Whether an act is right or wrong is to be judged according to its *consequences*. What are the consequences of an act of murder? Obviously, that someone is dead – but what has that to do with the greatest happiness principle? Try to think of an answer.●

One possible reply is that by murdering someone I lessen the amount of happiness around (because *he* is no longer around to be happy) or that I destroy the potential happiness he would have had if he had lived.

Another possible reply is that I cause suffering to his friends and relations.

I think that these are the only two replies a utilitarian can give. They both seem to me to be crazy grounds for saying that murder is wrong but, *even if they were right*, the utilitarian is still in difficulties. (b) Supposing the utilitarian has given either of those replies, or a combination of both, he still has a problem about saying why murder is wrong in certain cases. In certain cases he is going to be forced to say that murder is either permissible (i.e. *not* wrong) or, even worse, that it is morally obligatory and *right*. Can you see what these cases will be? (Is it clear what I am asking you to do? I am *not* asking you to think of cases where *you* might want to say that killing someone was not wrong on, for example, humanitarian grounds. I am asking you to think of cases where the utilitarian must, consistent with his grounds for calling murder wrong, say that in these circumstances it is not wrong, or even right. Preferably, these should be cases where most of us, since we are utilitarians only to *some* extent, not through and through, will say that in the circumstances murder is *wrong*.)●

SPECIMEN ANSWER

If what is wrong with murdering someone is that *he* is no longer around to be happy, either now or potentially, then, if I know someone is not happy and never is going to be happy, I might just as well murder him, if, say, it would give me pleasure, or save me some money, as long as it did not cause other people unhappiness.

If what is wrong with murdering someone is the unhappiness I cause his friends and relations, then someone without friends and relations, someone whose passing no-one will regret, is someone I may murder if I choose. Worse – it seems that if I know some miserable depressive person, who makes other people miserable, whose passing no-one will regret, who will never be happy himself and whose death will benefit many, then I *ought* to kill that person. It would be wrong of me, as a utilitarian, not to. (In Dostoyevsky's novel *Crime and Punishment*, the ⌈hero⌉ makes precisely that calculation about an old moneylender and murders her.)

I hope I have anticipated correctly at least the sorts of cases you have thought of. One sort of case I will just mention (it will be coming up later) that would also be a perfect answer here is any example involving a pure calculation of numbers. Suppose (ludicrously) there are six equally happy people with an equal number of loving friends and relations; one of the people is completely healthy, the others each lack one (different) essential bit: so why not kill the sixth and cut him up for the sake of the other five (on utilitarian grounds)?

On the strength of those examples, I conclude that utilitarianism cannot 'cope' with murder, by which I mean that there are some cases of murder which we think are wrong, which are *not* wrong *because* they violate the greatest happiness principle. Not all of them violate it; at least one, perhaps two, are actually in accordance with it. Some other moral principle or principles must be at work when we judge these acts to be wrong.

2.4.2 *Criminal unpunished*

Suppose that someone is found guilty of petty theft. The minimum penalty is a fine, but the offender argues that paying this fine will cause him and his family hardship and hence unhappiness, whereas if he is left unpunished then, as long as this is kept secret and no-one knows, no-one is made unhappy at all. If the judge is a utilitarian, how can he fail to agree with the offender? Surely he must let him go unpunished. What are your reactions to this example? Would they be different if I changed the nature of the crime? Think about this before reading on.●

DISCUSSION

You may have thought that the judge should let the offender go unpunished: that is, you may have reacted as a utilitarian. Suppose I substituted, for the crime of petty theft in the example, some really horrible crime. Choose your own example – would you still say that if the offender can argue that leaving him unpunished causes no harm, he ought to be allowed to go scot-free? We come at this point to a more general version of the problem. How can a utilitarian justify punishing criminals at all? Isn't punishing someone always a case of inflicting suffering on them? Even if it isn't, it certainly isn't promoting their happiness, and surely the utilitarian is committed to promoting the happiness of *everyone*, innocent and guilty alike, wherever possible. Can you think of what reply the utilitarian might make?●

The standard reply is that punishment, though an evil, is a necessary evil. The threat of it is needed to deter people from crime; and it must be inflicted in the case of crime to show that the threat is not an empty threat. This is a good reply, but it still leaves the utilitarian with a problem about punishment, which we will now go on to.

2.4.3 *Innocent punished*

The public prosecutor is prosecuting a man for robbery. The public prosecutor and the police know him to be a man who has committed many crimes, but never before have they managed to collect adequate evidence against him. When he is safely behind bars a number of people will be made much happier and safer, and no-one will regret his conviction. But the public prosecutor then discovers conclusive evidence that the man is, for once, innocent of this crime, the guilty party having confessed in a private letter and then having committed suicide. If the public prosecutor produces this evidence, not only will the man continue to terrorize and persecute his victims, but the real offender's family will suffer greatly. As a utilitarian, how can he do otherwise than keep quiet about the evidence and go ahead to condemn a man for a crime of which he is innocent? Once this is allowed, where can he draw the line? Perhaps on some other occasion the public interest, or happiness of many, will be best served by allowing a man innocent of *any* crime to be convicted. Perhaps a scapegoat is needed. But we have a strong moral principle according to which the innocent should never be punished. It is unjust to punish a man for a crime he did not commit.

2.4.4 *The examiner's case*

I am marking the exam. papers for a third level course and recognize the unmistakable handwriting and spelling of Jones. The paper is a clear F; but I know that Jones' assignment marks have been border-line, that if I mark the paper lower than C he will fail, that if he passes this unit he completes his BA and has been provisionally accepted to do a diploma which may well transform his life. No-one will double-check my marking;[1] no-one will ever know if I give him a

---

[1] Not true, fortunately!

mark he does not deserve. If I give him the correct mark of F, he suffers and no-one benefits; whereas if I give him a C, no-one suffers and he benefits enormously – and his family too. So as a utilitarian I *must* give him a C. There is not even room for doubt. Even if you don't agree with me (speaking now as a non-utilitarian) that it would be wrong of me to give him a C, I hope you will agree that there is at least room for doubt about its being obviously right to give him one.

2.4.5   *Promise-keeping*

This forms one of the largest sets of examples in discussions of utilitarianism and the arguments about various examples and theories have become, over the years, more and more elaborate. I hope you will soon see why. Once again, I am going to set out an extended argument in dialogue form and I want you to read it line by line, not looking ahead. Every now and then I'm going to ask you to guess how the next bit of the dialogue will go.

A: The utilitarian cannot account for the obligation to keep promises. If I have promised you I will do something – e.g. come to your party next week – then, when the time comes to do it, my decision about whether or not I ought to do it will have nothing to do with the fact that I promised you I would. Since it is a consequentialist doctrine, utilitarianism is forward-looking: it judges according to what will be the case, not according to what *has* happened. So it doesn't look backwards to the fact that I promised. It looks forward to the consequences of going or not going to your party. And if the consequences of going included, say, missing a much better party I could, as a utilitarian, judge that it was better not to come to yours. [B will criticize this; what will he say?]●

B: But if you *did* promise me, one of the consequences of not coming to my party will be having broken your promise. And that might be a bad consequence on utilitarian grounds.

A: I don't see how. [Can you? What will B say?]●

B   Well, it might make me unhappy, by disappointing me. By promising you created in me an expectation that you would come. If you hadn't promised then I might have been a bit sad you didn't come, but this might have been outweighed by how inconvenient it was for you to come. But since you *did* promise, you have to include in your calculations the fact that I will be more than a bit sad. I'll be very disappointed. [Did you get that one? There's another point B is going to make – about what he says to the other people at the party. Try to guess it.]●
     What's more, other people at the party may ask me whether you are coming. I will naturally say, 'Oh yes, he promised', and then if you don't show up, they will all know that you haven't kept your promise, and this will weaken their faith in you as a promise-keeper. You may find that people are ceasing to trust you, and that will make *you* unhappy. You will also find it very inconvenient.

A: Well, all right. I'll modify my position a little. How can a utilitarian cope with the following sort of example which eliminates the two factors you just brought up? [Can you produce an example before reading A's? Make sure that you are clear about *what* two factors are to be eliminated, and make sure your example really does eliminate them.]●
     I don't mind whether we call it the case of the desert-island promise, or the case of the death-bed promise. You can now probably guess the sort of example I have in mind. You and I are alone on a desert island or in a sick room. You ask me to promise to do something when you are dead – leave your money to a jockey club, educate your children, avenge your mother by tracking down the man who raped and killed her. I promise and subsequently you die. Assuming you can't look down from heaven, you are not around to be disappointed if I break the promise (which eliminates the first factor) and I am now the only person who knows that the promise was

made, so no-one's faith in me as a promise-keeper will be affected if I break it (which eliminates the second factor). If I break it, only I shall know. Well, I may, as a utilitarian, break it, or I may not. It will depend on the consequences of doing whatever it was I promised to do. But *that I promised* will have absolutely nothing to do with whether I do it or not. And that shows that in at least these cases the utilitarian cannot give any account of the obligation to keep a promise, because in these cases he says that the fact that I promised is absolutely irrelevant to deciding what I should do. [At this point B may give up; or he may make a last rather desperate attempt to save utilitarianism. He is going to say something about A's psychology. Can you guess what it is?]●

B: But *you* will know that you have broken your promise (if you do, that is). And won't that weaken your character as a habitual promise-keeper? Won't it make you more likely to break promises in the future, when doing so would *not* have good consequences? Once you get into the habit, you'll just go round breaking promises all the time. [What will A say to that? It's a very common-sense reply.]●

A: Look, doing it *once*, in these extraordinary and very artificial circumstances, is hardly getting into a habit. Don't let's get carried away.

B: All right, but you are running a risk, aren't you? Perhaps a very small risk, but there's a *chance* that breaking this promise might start you off down the slippery slope to being a habitual promise-breaker.

A: Well, so what? You surely aren't going to say that this shows that on utilitarian grounds I must always keep my promises, because there's always a small risk I might be starting on the slippery slope. *Always*?

B   (remembering that he is a utilitarian): Well, no. As a utilitarian I must of course agree that no moral rule, such as 'Keep promises', is sacrosanct. But you did say that in the case of the death-bed or desert-island promise, the *promise* makes no difference when it comes to making up your mind what to do.

A: I'll say three things: (i) I'll concede to you that in *theory* it makes a bit of a difference; (ii) I'll emphasize that in *practice*, since we are talking about such a ludicrously remote chance and such a small if not negligible risk, it would never be a consideration of sufficient weight to tip a balance and (iii) I'll remind you that the sort of difference it makes in theory is not going to satisfy the opponents of utilitarianism. They want an account of the obligation to keep promises. They want an account of why it is that 'I promised *Jones* I would, so I owe it to him to do so' is a moral reason. We have not managed to do any better than 'I promised I would (no matter to whom the promise is made), so perhaps I should do it in case not doing it weakens my character.' Where does *Jones* and my obligation to *him* figure in that? [End of dialogue.]

2.4.6   *Anti-social acts*

You may have thought of a reply on B's behalf which I did not allow him to make. I was saving it for the next dialogue. I now want us to run through a similar argument about the 'Why shouldn't I? It suits me and it does no harm' examples. The same instructions apply as in the last dialogue, and once again A begins by raising an objection to utilitarianism, and B is going to be the person defending it.

A: There is a whole class of cases which we think of as cases of doing something wrong – not perhaps really wicked, but quite wrong or at least anti-social. The utilitarian account seems to yield the counterintuitive conclusion that these acts are not even often wrong (as perhaps torture, murder and promise-breaking are) but usually right!

B: Which ones are you thinking of?

A: The ones mentioned in (6) on page 66 above. Let's take picking flowers from public parks. Suppose I'm in a park in spring, surrounded by hundreds and hundreds of daffodils. I live in a small dark bed-sitter, whose window looks out on a wall, with a friend who is sick. If I picked a bunch of daffodils it would be nice for me; it would be really nice for her and cheer her up, and it would do no harm. So why shouldn't I do it? It seems that on utilitarian grounds I *ought* to do it; that it would be the right thing to do.

B: What makes you so sure it does no harm?

A: What harm do you think it would do? [What will B reply?]●

B: The whole point of having flowers in a public park is that everyone can look at them and enjoy them. If you take the flowers away you are depriving other people, lots of other people, of the pleasure of looking at them, just to give two people pleasure, yourself and your friend. [What does A reply?]●

A: I agree that it would be wrong to strip the whole park *bare*, but I wasn't suggesting that I went home with a lorry-load of daffodils. I said there were hundreds and hundreds and I pick *one* bunch. [What does B say now?]●

B: But each one you pick might have given someone pleasure. Suppose you pick twenty: that's twenty units less of happiness potentially in the park. [What does A say? *Very* common-sense and down-to-earth.]●

A: I must insist that we talk sense and not gibberish. A daffodil is not a unit of pleasure or happiness. There are indeed no such things as units of pleasure or happiness and it is silly to talk as if there were. Could you find a less exceptionable way of making your point, please?

B: All right, the point is this. Even if you take no more than twenty from thousands, you still take some and so there are fewer than there were before, right? So there are fewer to enjoy, right? *That's* the harm you do. [What does A say?]●

A: You mean the people who look at the, say, 1,980 daffodils don't get as much pleasure from the sight as they would have got from looking at 2,000?

B: Right. [What does A say?]●

A: Wrong. Do you think there's anyone who can spot the difference between a field of 1,980 daffodils and a field of 2,000? I don't think there is.

B: All right, I expect there isn't. But all the same, if 1,980 daffodils give . . .

A: *Don't* say units.

B: . . . if they give a certain amount of pleasure, more daffodils must give more pleasure. [This is obviously false and A will give a counter-example. Can you think of one?]●

A: If you think about that seriously, I think you will admit that it is just not true. One mass of daffodils does not in *fact* give more pleasure than an indiscriminably larger mass and to say that they *must*, as though it were some kind of mathematical law, is to misapply mathematical laws and is just silly. 2,000 daffodils must weigh more than that same mass minus 20; they must occupy more space; but it doesn't follow that they must give more pleasure. You might just as well say – [try again to think of a counter-example if you haven't yet]●
– you might just as well say that eating twenty pounds of steak at a sitting must give more pleasure than eating one pound; or that drinking five bottles of whisky in an evening must give more pleasure than drinking two glasses. And that's obviously not true. The first would make you sick and the second would probably kill you. So let's abandon that nonsensical line. Try again. *What* harm am I going to do by picking those flowers? [Any offers on B's behalf?]●

B: Well, someone might see you. Or someone might notice the ends of the stalks and realize that someone had picked some of the flowers.

A: I'm picking the flowers in the middle of an empty park; I can *see* it's empty. I pick them from the middle of clumps so that you can't see the stalk ends.

B: But all the same, someone *might* see. You are still running *some* risk.

A: All right. Suppose someone did see me picking the flowers, or did see the stalks. So what?

B: Then they might pick bunches of daffodils too, encouraged by your example. [A's reply?]●

A: They *might*. But then, on the other hand, they might not. They might have been thinking of doing so and then be put off by realizing that someone else had.

B: All the same, you are still running *some* risk.

A: This is becoming tedious. Are you telling me that it's wrong to pick flowers from public parks when it looks empty to me and so on, because there's a remote chance that someone might see me, and that in that unlikely case there's a further remote chance that he might be tempted to do the same and then there's a similarly remote chance that someone might see him . . .

B: That's right. There's always a risk, however remote, so it's wrong.

A: Well, *if* that were true, all sorts of perfectly innocuous and innocent actions would be wrong. It would probably be wrong ever to stir outside one's own home.

B: Why? [Can you see why? Remember to relate it to B's last remark above.]●

A: *If* it's wrong to run the most minimal and remote chance of doing harm, it is *certainly* wrong ever to drive a car, since the risk of doing harm is more than minimal; it's wrong to ride a bicycle, since you *might* cause an accident, and even in walking to the local shops you might, you just might, bump into someone with a weak heart. 'There's always a risk, however remote, so it's wrong.'

B: That's just silly.

A: I couldn't agree more. But it's what you said, not what I wanted to say.

B: All right. I admit I made a mistake. But all the same it's surely wrong to pick flowers from public parks.

A: Surely. But can a *utilitarian* consistently maintain that it is wrong?

B: Well, what is wrong about it *does* have to do with its consequences in accordance with the greatest-happiness principle. I mean, if everyone went around picking flowers from public parks there would be no flowers and so people wouldn't be able to enjoy looking at them. And certainly from the utilitarian point of view, that's a bad thing. – Yes! That's it! That's what is wrong with *all* those cases you mentioned. The individual act does not itself do any harm, but the point is that they are all the sorts of acts which, if everyone did them, would have disastrous consequences. If everyone picked the flowers there would be no flowers, if everyone dropped litter the whole country would be filthy, if everyone rips off the big businesses the prices go up and we get inflation, and the same with not paying bus fares; if everyone walks on the grass it wears out the grass, and so on. [End of dialogue.]●

If you had already thought of this new manoeuvre of B's, that's very good: it is quite a famous refinement on basic utilitariansim and is the next thing I'm going

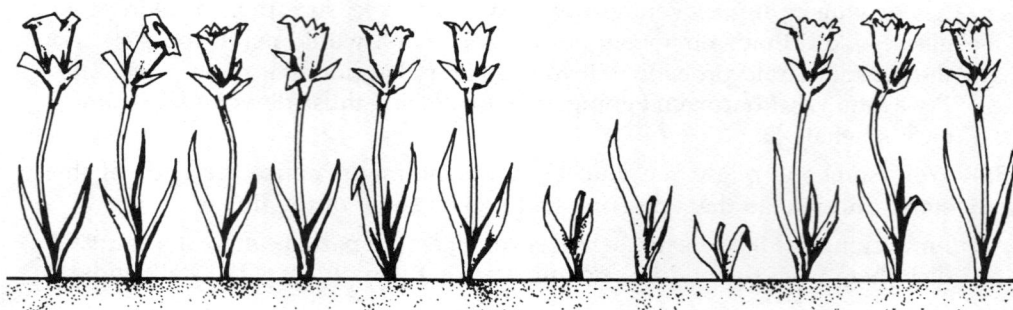

to discuss. If you didn't think of it, don't worry; it took philosophers a long time to think of it after Mill.

Before you read on I should like you to try to answer two questions:

1 Does this new manoeuvre of B's help to solve any of the other problems utilitarianism is faced with? If so, how? (Try it on just one problem.)
2 And how can it cope with the down-to-earth reply, 'But not everyone *is* going to do it, so why shouldn't *I*, since doing it does no harm?'

Try to write about 100–200 words on this before reading on. ●

2.5 RULE AND ACT UTILITARIANISM

I'm not going to give a specimen answer to those questions. I just wanted to get you involved in the discussion, and if you have thought *hard* about those questions you will have learned as much as you would have from reading three or four articles in philosophical journals on the subject. If you have thought hard about the questions you will be familiar with the problems involved and that should make the following discussion easier for you to follow.

B has produced a famous refinement on basic utilitarianism, which is known as *rule* or restricted utilitarianism, as opposed to *act* or extreme utilitarianism. Act utilitarianism is so called because, according to it, we apply the utilitarian principle to the consequences of the *act* itself and judge the rightness or wrongness of the act thereby. According to rule utilitarianism we apply the utilitarian principle to the hypothetical consequences of everyone following a *rule* that such and such an act is to be done or not done. We thereby judge the rightness or wrongness of the rule and, derivatively, the rightness or wrongness of particular acts. An act is right if it falls under a right rule. A rule enjoining such acts is right if and only if the consequences of everyone's doing such acts would promote the greatest happiness.[1]

That is perhaps not perfectly clear. It is hard to state rule utilitarianism clearly in the abstract. Let me put it another way. Suppose I am a rule utilitarian and I'm trying to decide whether it would be right for me to do something – e.g. take a short cut across the grass. I *don't* apply the utilitarian principle to the consequences of the act itself. (Then I would be an act utilitarian.) Instead, I ask myself the question 'What would be the consequences of everyone following a rule, "Walk across the grass when it suits you"?' That is, I ask myself the question 'What if everybody did that?' Well, the consequences would certainly not promote the greatest happiness, because the grass would get an ugly path worn across it. So the rule is not a right rule. So the act is not right.

Act and rule utilitarians regard the question 'But what if everybody did that?' quite differently. For an act utilitarian it is merely one question among many about the possible consequences of his act, and usually not a question that needs to be asked. To him it means 'Will I cause everyone to do the same, if I do such and such? And *if* so, what then?' This question is not significantly different from lots of others: 'Will I cause Jim to do the same, if I do such and such? And if so, what then?' 'Will I prevent Jane from doing so and so if I do such and such? And if so, what then?' These are all questions about possible consequences of the act. In each case, if the answer to the first bit of the question is 'No', the act utilitarian can forget about the second bit. Will he cause Jim to do the same? No? Then he needn't worry about 'And if so, what then?' Will he prevent Jane from doing so and so? No? Then he needn't worry about 'And if so, what then?' Will he cause everybody to do whatever it is, if he does it? No? Then he can forget about the question.

---

[1] When an act falls under two different right rules, one enjoining it and the other forbidding it, we are allowed to apply the principle directly to the act itself, just as an act utilitarian would.

Obviously, the question 'Will I cause everyone to do the same, if I do so and so?' is not a question that many of us need to ask very often. Most of us do not have that sort of influence. It is so obvious that *my* watering my garden during the water shortage, *my* picking flowers from public parks, *my* dropping litter and so on, isn't going to cause everybody else to do it, that I don't need to consider the question. It's just irrelevant. As an act utilitarian, I am interested only in actual consequences.

There is no point in saying to an act utilitarian, 'But what if everybody *did* do that', in the hope that it will stop him doing such things. He may agree that '*If* everybody did that, the consequences would be bad' but he will not see that as a reason for refraining from such acts. As long as he knows that he will not cause everyone to do that, he can still go ahead and do it.

For the rule utilitarian, on the other hand, the question 'But what if everybody did that?' is *the* moral question. He does not just ask it on the rare occasions when he is likely to cause everybody to do what he does. He asks it on every occasion on which he is judging as to the rightness or wrongness of acts. For him the fact (if it is a fact) that on some occasion it is certain that not everyone *is* going to do whatever it is, is irrelevant. He is not concerned with actual consequences, but with the hypothetical consequences of everyone's, hypothetically, doing whatever it is.

How do you think act and rule utilitarians respectively will regard moral rules such as 'Keep promises', 'Tell the truth', 'Thou shalt not kill' and so on? Jot down a couple of sentences for each before reading on.●

DISCUSSION

For the act utilitarian, moral rules (Keep promises! Don't steal!) are rules of thumb. When you have to act in a hurry and don't have time to weigh up the consequences; when things are very complicated and it is extremely difficult to work out what all the consequences of your act will be; when you suspect that for one reason or another – because you are tired, ill, mentally disturbed, emotionally involved – you will not make an unbiased or unprejudiced judgement about the probable consequences; when any of those apply, *then* following the moral rules is the best bet. But, as an act utilitarian, you do not follow the rule because following the rule is doing the right thing. Doing the right thing is doing the thing that promotes the greatest happiness and you follow the rule in the hope that on this occasion it will, as it often does, lead to the right result.

For the rule utilitarian, certain rules are sacrosanct in *theory*, but in practice it is difficult to determine what these rules are. The rule utilitarian should certainly not be condemned as an unthinking moral conservative who erects rules into some kind of idol to be worshipped. Some philosophers have condemned rule utilitarianism on those grounds, but I suspect this is because they have thought of the problem in over-simplified terms. Let's make sure we don't make the same mistake.

Consider, for instance, the rule 'Keep promises.' At first sight, it seems that the rule utilitarian will maintain that this is an exceptionless rule. Breaking promises is wrong because if everyone went round breaking their promises the whole institution of promise-keeping would break down and that would certainly not promote the greatest happiness. But if we make the rule sacrosanct we get landed with a problem. Can you see what it is?●

If we make the rule sacrosanct, we make keeping promises ludicrously important. Suppose that I have not only promised to come to your party but promised to arrive early to help get things ready. On my way I pass someone having a heart attack; no-one else is around. If I stop to ring an ambulance or drive the person to the nearest hospital I shan't arrive in time to help you get things ready. And so I drive on!

That's obviously silly. Keeping a promise about coming to a party is nothing like as important as saving someone's life. The rule utilitarian is not committed to anything so absurd. What reply does he make?•

He has two replies. He can point out that 'Preserve life' is certainly a good moral rule on his test and that the preceding example is a case in which an act falls under two moral rules. He has already agreed that when we get a clash of rules we appeal directly to the greatest happiness principle. So in this case he and the act utilitarian will agree about what ought to be done. Of course the promise should be broken, and the life saved.

He has another, more subtle, reply, which is to complicate his rule. He can say (a) that it is *true* that if everyone went round breaking their promises all the time the institution of promise-keeping would break down and (b) that it is *false* that if everyone always kept their promises, regardless of the consequences, this would promote the greatest happiness and (c) that there is a midway position. If everyone always kept their promises *except* when, e.g., doing so would cause a great deal of harm or when breaking them would do a great deal of good, then the institution of promise-keeping would *not* break down and the greatest happiness *would* be promoted.

Ideally this should mean that the rule and act utilitarian agree on the obvious cases, and still disagree on the cases where most of us want to side against the act utilitarian. (E.g. when, as an act utilitarian, I break a death-bed promise because it suits me.)

So, rule utilitarianism does not require that we erect our simple rules like 'Keep promises' into idols, but it shows them more respect than act utilitarianism and hence seems to avoid some of the problems utilitarianism was faced with. Let's run through the others. Turn back to page 66 and run through them yourself.•

It copes with murder by saying that if everyone went round killing everyone soon there wouldn't be any people left and that would really put paid to the greatest happiness for the greatest number. It says that the judge cannot let the criminal go unpunished, nor the public prosecutor let the innocent man be punished, because as a general practice this would undermine our whole system of law, which does, on the whole, work for the good. Similarly, passing people because they need to pass undermines the whole examination system, breaking promises when it suits you undermines the institution of promise-keeping, and we have already been through the cases of picking flowers from public parks when we started this discussion.

So far, it looks as though rule utilitarianism does solve all the problems. Are you convinced? Or do you think it is right in some cases but wrong in others?•

2.6   PROBLEMS FOR RULE UTILITARIANISM

I think it is right over some things but completely wrong over others. The cases I think it's wrong over are the ones where it yields an acceptable result, but for the wrong reasons. That is, it yields the result 'We ought not to do so and so' but if we ask *why*, the moral reason given just is not the right one. It's completely artificial. That's what I think. Now I'll give some examples.

Two men are stranded on a desert island; they have enough food to feed one until the rescue boat arrives but if they share, both will die. One man is a widower who has led a solitary life, whose children hardly know him. He knows that the other man has a wife and children who will be very unhappy if he dies. The first man therefore offers to sacrifice his life, asking that the second man will, in return, look after and educate his children. He signs a document handing over his modest fortune. Then he dies and the other man goes back and breaks the promise on the grounds that the other man's children are getting by on the money left them by their mother and that he can do a lot more for his wife and his own children, who are harder up.

Now do you think that what is wrong with what that man did is that if - everyone - went - around - breaking - promises - like - that - the - whole - institution - of - promise - keeping - would - break - down? I think what he did was very wrong, but not for *that* reason.

I take one healthy man off the street and kill him to cut him up to save five. Do you think that what is wrong with that is that if - it - were - a - general - practice - we - should - all - feel - desperately - insecure - all - the - time? Or that if - it - were - a - general - practice - the - race - would - soon - die - out - because - the - healthy - would - have - been - killed - to - preserve - the - unhealthy? I think it is wrong but not for either of those reasons.

After one of my kindest and most generous friends dies, I find that, despite the fact that I have neglected him shamefully for the last ten years, he has left me everything in his will, together with a most touching tribute to my love and loyalty. This makes me feel very guilty and to rid myself of the guilt I pretend to myself that he wasn't so marvellous after all. Seeking to make other people think the same I tell a very mean lie about him – say that he indulged in really filthy practices (think of your own example if that one doesn't suit you). Do you think that what is wrong with telling that lie is that the consequences of everyone's telling horrid lies about people after they are dead would be very bad? Well, that isn't even clear. After all, if everyone did it, we would all know that stories about the dead weren't true, so it would all cancel out and not matter at all.

It seems to me that all the acts I have described are unmistakably wrong, but *not* wrong for the reasons a rule utilitarian must give. (Nor are they wrong for any reasons an act utilitarian might try to give either.) The first is wrong because it is a betrayal of trust. The second is wrong because, minimally, though perhaps for other reasons as well, it is violating someone's right to life, and the third is wrong because it is mean, low, grudging and ungrateful.[1]

On the other hand, what is wrong with dropping litter, picking flowers from public parks, etc. *in* the circumstances where it really does no harm is, I think, precisely captured by rule utilitarianism. It's wrong *because* if - everybody - did - that - whenever - they - wanted - to - we - wouldn't - have - clean - parks - with - green - lawns - and - flowers.

2.7   CONCLUSION

Do we want to bring up our children to do and refrain from certain sorts of acts, or do we want to bring them up to be certain sorts of people? The trouble with bringing them up to do and refrain from certain sorts of acts is finding the right way to describe the acts, or specifying the rules we want the children to grow up following. We have seen that we don't simply want to bring them up blindly

[1] This is one of the two points I want you to get out of the *'Jumpers'* programme (Television Programme 14), where it is put across very vividly. Describing the views of McPhee (obviously a rule-utilitarian), George says, '. . . he believes that on the whole people should tell the truth and keep their promises, and so on – but on the sole grounds that if everyone went round telling lies and breaking their word then normal life would be impossible. Telling lies is not *sinful* but simply anti-social . . .' And this applies equally to murder. George's own criticism of this view isn't particularly interesting, but Bones puts his finger unerringly on what is ludicrous about it when he says, incredulously: 'He thinks there's nothing *wrong* with killing people!?!' Rule utilitarianism is ludicrous applied to murder, though absolutely right applied to anti-social acts.

following the rule 'Act so as to promote the greatest happiness.' Then they would grow up as act utilitarians and do some horrible things. We don't want to bring them up as blind rule-followers, keeping promises at the expense of someone's life. We don't even want to bring them up to be sophisticated rule utilitarians, who modify their rules in careful ways, or at least I don't, because they will be doing the right things for the wrong reasons and I cannot predict when those same wrong reasons will, as they might, lead to horrible conclusions. Don't we want our children to be utilitarians at all, then?

Surely we do. We want utilitarian considerations to be *amongst* their moral considerations. We want them to be humanitarian – to rejoice in human happiness and be appalled by human suffering. We want them to be the sort of people who see 'It will promote happiness', 'It will spare him suffering' as reasons for acting, and who see 'It will make him unhappy' and 'It will make him suffer' as reasons for refraining. Not as the *only* reasons for acting or refraining, but as reasons amongst others. In that sense we want them to be *act* utilitarians.

But we do not want them to be exclusively individualistic. We want them, by and large, to be public-spirited or community-minded, prepared to act as part of a community effort without being able to see immediate actual consequences of acting well, but content to be a small cog in a large machine. To this extent, we want them to be rule utilitarians. In certain areas, they should see 'If everyone contributes, we'll wind up with good results' as a reason for acting and 'If everybody did that, the consequences would be bad' as a reason for refraining. Not the *only* reasons, but reasons amongst others. So we want them to react to the remark 'Not everyone *is* going to do that' differently, according to circumstances. Sometimes they should react by saying, 'Oh good; then I'll go ahead' and sometimes they should react by saying, 'So what? What everyone *actually* does is not the point.'

A lot of modern moral philosophy is bedevilled by a mania for oversimplification. First of all philosophers try to cram all of our moral reasoning into the utilitarian mould and then, as if that weren't bad enough, try to contort it into *either* pure act *or* pure rule utilitarianism. The aim is praiseworthy. The aim is to guarantee that there is always a simple straightforward answer to the question 'What ought I to do on this occasion?' But life, unfortunately, is not so simple; there *are* genuine moral dilemmas where there is no simple answer. The philosopher who ignores this fact

> . . . would be the lunatic of one idea
> In a world of ideas, who would have all the people
> Live, work, suffer and die in that idea
> In a world of ideas. He would not be aware of the clouds
> Lighting the martyrs of logic with white fire,
> His extreme of logic would be illogical.
>
> (Wallace Stevens) 'Esthétique du Mal'

IN CASE YOU LOSE YOUR MASKING CARD

(a) *A value judgement* is, roughly, a judgement in which a value word is used.

(b) *A value judgement* is a judgement in which the speaker somehow indicates, expresses, conveys, implies, suggests, or gives away what his preferences, likes or dislikes (roughly, values), are.

(c) *A subjective judgement* is a judgement which is not strictly in accordance with the facts.

(d) *A subjective judgement* is a judgement a person makes *because* he is biased, prejudiced and/or influenced by personal feelings.

(e) *A subjective judgement* is a judgement in which the speaker says something about himself as a thinking thing, or as a person.

NB In this context 'the speaker' is a quasi-technical term. It means the person who makes the judgement, regardless of whether he says it – that is, speaks – or says it in a book, or makes it to himself. 'The judger' is not English; 'the promulgator of the judgement' is ludicrously heavy, so we use 'the speaker'.

UNIT 15 SCEPTICISM AND SENSE-DATA

CONTENTS

INTRODUCTION

In Unit 13 I mentioned scepticism about the external world several times. I had the sceptic saying, 'How do you know there was anyone at the door? Perhaps your senses were deceiving you, perhaps you were hallucinating. All you can be certain of is that you seemed to see a man at the door', and so on. I said several times that I had done no more than sketch his arguments and that we would be going into the problem more thoroughly in Unit 15.

This we are now going to do. You are now going to be introduced to your third standard philosophical problem, namely the problem of our knowledge of the external world. But any philosopher who assumes, reasonably enough, that *perception* is a necessary and fundamental condition of this knowledge, sees the problem as inextricably involved with another, or others, namely, the problem or problems of perception. Hence this unit is as much about perception as it is about knowledge.

I should like you to feel that you had made real progress by the time you reach the end of this unit, but it would be ludicrous to expect that the real progress consisted in your knowing all about perception and knowledge. No-one could write a unit which would achieve that. I am aiming for something more modest.

In a minute, I shall ask you to read the extract from Russell on pp. 94–95 of your *Supplementary Texts*. I want you to read it carefully, perhaps more than once, and to make a note of anything you object to in it, or find puzzling. After you have read it a couple of times and made your notes, would you please put it away and

Figure 1   Bertrand Russell (1872–1970)

forget about it until you have read the unit. At the end of the unit, I shall ask you to read it again. If this unit succeeds in its modest aim, you will find your understanding of the extract enormously increased, and this, I hope, will convince you that you have made real progress. Let me make two things absolutely clear:

1   The unit is *not* about the Russell extract. That's one reason why I want you to put the extract away and forget about it after you have read it the first couple of times. I talk at some length about some points which do not come up in the Russell at all, and if you keep on referring back to it and asking yourself, 'But where does that point come up in this extract?' you will only get muddled. The unit *is* about our knowledge of the external world and perception. So is the Russell extract and of course there is *some* overlap, but don't go hunting for the overlap.

2   The point of reading the extract is to give yourself a sort of 'Before' and 'After' way of measuring your own progress. If your reaction to the extract 'Before' and 'After' reading this unit is the same both times then the unit has failed (or you are a natural born philosopher!). But, as I said above, I hope you will find that your understanding of the extract has increased enormously.

Please will you read the Russell extract *now*.●

1 RELYING ON OUR SENSES

1.1 INTRODUCTION

Consider the following dialogue.

A: How do you come by your knowledge of the world around you? How do you know that there is a book in front of you, a chair underneath you, wine in your glass, onions frying in the kitchen, an OU programme on the wireless? Through pure reason?

B: No, of course not. Through perception, or, as some philosophers say, sense-experience. I have five senses – touch, sight, hearing, taste and smell – and by means of them I perceive the physical world. I know there's a book in front of me because I can see it; I can see the wine in my glass and I just tasted it so I know it's wine; I can smell the onions, hear the OU programme, feel the chair underneath me.

A: And how do you know what these things are like (what properties or qualities they have, what is true of them)?

B: The same way a lot of the time. I know the cover of the book is red and shiny because I can see that it is. I can feel that the seat of the chair is soft and the desk top is hard. I know the wine is sweet because I just tasted it, and so on.

A: So you think you know pretty much what the world is really like?

B: Yes.

A: But aren't you relying on your senses for that knowledge?

B: Well, why shouldn't I?

That is a good aggressive question of B's. Some philosophers have answered it by saying that we shouldn't rely on our senses because they are not reliable. Their supposed unreliability is supposedly proved by appeal to illusions and hallucinations. (Notice how cautious I am being about whether the senses are really unreliable, or have really been proved to be.) Before going on to the next section see if you can think of some examples of illusions or hallucinations which you think *might* be used to show that our senses are unreliable.●

1.2 ILLUSIONS AND HALLUCINATIONS

Most philosophers who describe themselves as writing about perception, wind up writing almost exclusively about sight. This is undoubtedly in *part* because sight provides so many fascinating examples of illusions and hallucinations. But it is possible to find a few examples relating to the other senses. One of the most famous concerns touch. A lukewarm bath may feel cold to one hand (which has just been in a fur glove) and hot to the other (which has just been in iced water). Another old example (used by Plato!) concerns taste; wine which tastes sweet when I have just eaten cheese, tastes sour when I have just eaten strawberry shortcake. Hearing: as the train rushes towards me I hear the pitch of its whistle go higher as the train approaches and then go lower again as the train passes; but of course the people on the train hear the whistle at a constant pitch.

And so to sight. There are many illusions concerning movement. Amongst the most ordinary everyday ones are the way the moon appears to sail through the sky when clouds are scudding across its face; and the way the train you are *in* appears to be moving when you look out the window at the train which is leaving from the *next* platform. One everyday example concerning size is that the moon looks bigger when it is near the horizon than it does when it is right above you. More extraordinary examples have been invented by psychologists.

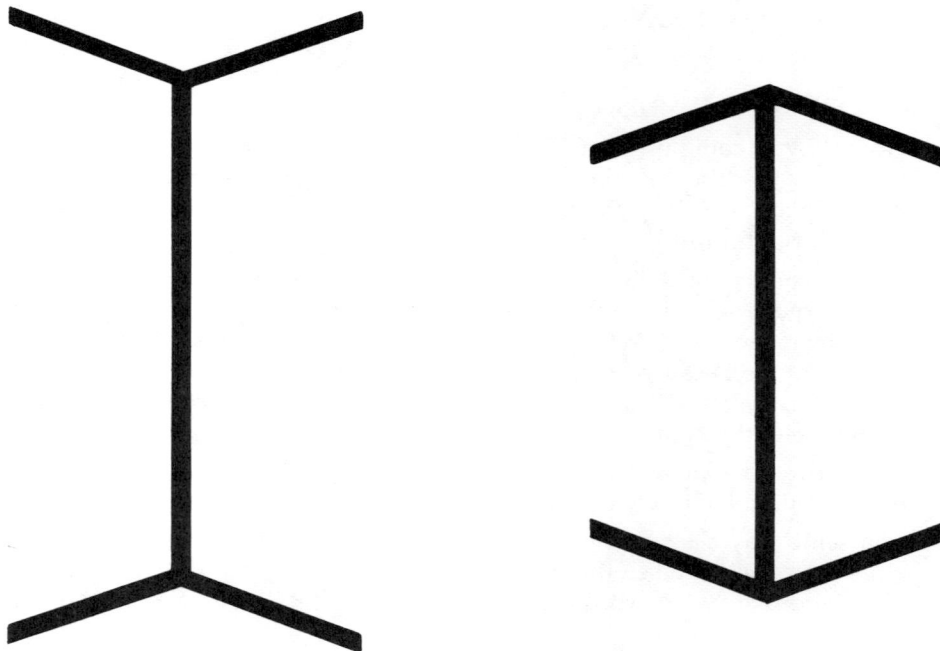

Figure 2   The Müller–Lyer figure

Figure 2 is known as the Müller–Lyer figure; as you can find out by using a ruler, the upright lines are of equal length but, unless you are *very* unusual, they will look unequal.

Figure 3   Ames' distorted room

In Figure 3, there are no giants. This illusion is produced by building a specially distorted room. Its real shape is shown in Figure 4.

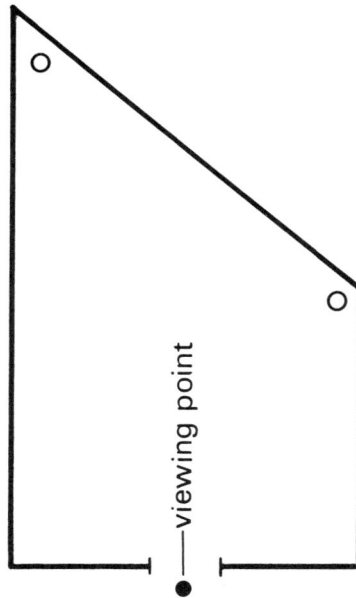

Figure 4   The real shape of Ames' distorted room

Another example philosophers often give is *mirages*, about which a word is necessary. Some people do not know that mirages are *not* necessarily imaginary pictures of lush green places filled with fountains and naked houris that you see in the desert because you are crazed with thirst. Mirages can be *photographed* (Figure 5). They are a phenomenon of light, like mirror images and rainbows.

Figure 5   Photograph of the Canigou mountain seen from Marseilles, silhouetted against the setting sun. The mountain is actually below the horizon and can only be seen because the light rays follow a curved path round the surface of the earth

The reason they are associated with deserts is that they are phenomena which can be caused by the air's being hot. The trees which are actually beyond the horizon appear located (and can be photographed) on the horizon as a result of the bending of light waves by layers of hot air. A similar phenomenon occurs on roads on hot days. The heat from the road bends the light waves in such a way that we see a reflection of the sky. We may mistake it for a pool of water, but we don't see it *just* because we are hot and want water. It too can be photographed.

These mirages which *can* be photographed should be contrasted with what I shall call (not illusions but) hallucinations, which are the cases when you perceive something that isn't there at all. People crazed with heat and thirst in the desert, or indeed at sea, have reported hallucinating extraordinary things. It is said, though I do not know with what truth, that people suffering from delirium tremens (DT's) see either pink rats or pink elephants. It is certainly true that people in delirium, or under the influence of the advisedly named 'hallucinogenic' drugs such as LSD, perceive things that are not there.

The best description of a hallucinatory experience is from Shakespeare – the example is always referred to simply as 'Macbeth's dagger'.

Macbeth: Is this a dagger which I see before me,
The handle toward my hand? Come let me clutch thee:
I have thee not, and yet I see thee still.
Art thou not, fatal vision, sensible
To feeling as to sight? or art thou but
A dagger of the mind, a false creation,
Proceeding from the heat-oppressed brain?

('Sensible to feeling' means 'able to be sensed by feeling', i.e. 'able to be felt.')

Finally, a non-fictional and fascinating example known as the 'phantom-limb phenomenon'. Apparently it is quite common for people who have had a limb amputated to continue to feel pains and sometimes other sensations, *in the missing limb*, sometimes for many years! Even when they know it has gone they are inclined to forget and sometimes try to rub, or scratch an itch in, a place which has no leg or arm in it!

1.3   WHAT DOES THEIR EXISTENCE PROVE?

It seems beyond reasonable doubt that there are illusions and hallucinations. We *know* that on certain occasions 'the testimony of our senses', as it is called, is not to be relied on. We *know* that on certain occasions our senses are unreliable.

Does it follow that we should not rely on them? Does it follow that we cannot claim to know anything on the basis of sense-experience? What do you think?●

Something ought to strike you as funny about drawing the conclusion that we cannot claim to know anything on the basis of sense-experience from the premise that we know that on certain occasions our senses are unreliable. Can you see something fishy about it?●

If not, ask yourself the question, '*How* do we know that on certain occasions, such as those described in section 1.2, our senses are unreliable?' Can you see something fishy now? Whether you can or can't, would you please now read lines 73–119 of the second Ayer extract on page 80 of your *Supplementary Texts*.●

DISCUSSION

The answer to the question 'How do we know that on certain occasions such as those described in section 1.2, our senses are unreliable?' is – 'Through our senses.'

So the fishy argument goes like this: 'Through our senses, we know that on *certain* occasions our senses are unreliable. So they are unreliable. So we can't know anything through them.'

When it is written out like that we can see clearly what is wrong with it. It undercuts itself. *If* we can't know anything through our senses *then* we can't know that on certain occasions they are unreliable. And if we can't know that, bang goes the premise of the argument.

So what does follow from the fact that there are illusions and hallucinations? What does their existence prove? Well, it proves that our senses are not *infallible* (but surely no-one ever thought they were). And at least some of the examples suggest that perceiving is a complex business – more complex than perhaps one had initially supposed.

Comprehension questions on this section

Question 1

A: This bath is cold at one end and warm at the other!

B: How do you know?

A: Well this end, where I put my left hand, feels cold, and this end, where I put my right hand, feels warm.

B: Were your hands at ordinary temperature?

A: I shouldn't think so. I've just been outside, and though I kept my left hand really warm, I had to take the glove off my right hand to feel around in the tank of icy water.

B: I don't think you should claim to know the bathwater is different temperatures. I doubt very much that it is.

Is B's doubt reasonable?●

ANSWER

Yes, it is. If A asked why he doubted (i.e. what his *grounds* for doubting were) B could give an answer.

Question 2
What answer could he give?●

SPECIMEN ANSWER

He could say, 'You know perfectly well that when your hands are very hot or very cold, things don't feel their real temperature. How things feel to your hands when your hands are abnormally hot or abnormally cold is a bad guide to how they are.' He *could* also say, 'I doubt that the bathwater is different temperatures, because I know that it isn't. I just put my hand in and swished it around both ends and the whole bath is lukewarm.' Let's suppose he really did do that. Now the dialogue goes on . . .

Question 3

A: Are you saying you *know* the bathwater is lukewarm?

B: Yes.

A: Well, I doubt *that*; I don't think you *can* know.

Is A's doubt reasonable?●

DISCUSSION

If you have said 'No!' then that shows you have got the general idea and that's excellent. But saying 'No!' straight off is a *little* incautious. Are you quite sure A's doubt must be unreasonable? (Remember that we haven't been told much about A and B.) What is the cautious answer to Question 3?●

DISCUSSION CONTINUED

The cautious answer is something like this. A's doubt *might* be reasonable, if, for instance he knows that there is something special about B or about the bath-water. He might say, 'You can't know – not by feeling the water with that artificial hand, anyhow.' But it seems more likely that A is being sceptical. He is not casting *reasonable* doubt on B's claim to know that the bathwater is lukewarm; he is not pointing out that the ordinary justification for such claims has not (yet) been given. Rather, he is saying that the ordinary justification for such claims is not good enough. Let's suppose he makes this obvious.

Question 4

A: You can't say you really *know* the bathwater is lukewarm because you tested it with your hand. That's not good enough – it's just relying on your senses.

B: Well, what's wrong with doing that?

A: You know perfectly well that our senses are not reliable. Why, you yourself just pointed out that I couldn't go by how things felt when my hands were abnormal temperatures. You *know* we can't rely on our senses. You *agreed* with that.

What's wrong with what A has just said?●

SPECIMEN ANSWER

What B had pointed out and agreed to was that we know our senses are *sometimes* not reliable, or that they are *not always* reliable. To move from this point to saying we know they are at *all times* not reliable, or *never* reliable, would be to make a rash generalization. It would also be self-refuting. For *how* do we know that our senses are sometimes not reliable? According to what A and B are agreed on, we know through our senses. So (sometimes) they *are* to be relied on.

1.4   MORE ILLUSIONS. ARE WE VERY LIKELY TO BE WRONG WHEN RELYING ON WHAT WE SEE?

There is a large set of examples other than those I have mentioned which are often used in an attempt to show that our senses (well, in these cases, just sight) are *deceptive*. Here are some of them:

When I look at a round penny (an old penny) from most angles it looks elliptical. My house on the horizon looks no bigger than a matchbox. When I look at a rectangular table from most angles it looks sort of diamond-shaped, as if it had two acute angles and two obtuse angles. When I look at myself in the mirror, my body appears to be some distance behind the glass. When I look at something shiny it appears to have white streaks or stripes on it. The green grass, purple heather, grey rock on the distant mountainside all look blue or purple. A straight stick in water looks bent. The vane in Television Programme 15 appears to change direction.

(Before reading on, think briefly about these examples. If some of them seem different from others, make a note of it. If you can say *why* they seem different, all the better. For instance, do you think 'looks' and 'appears' are being used in

90

the same way in all the examples? As you will know if you have seen Television Programme 15 (or will find out, when you do see it), a distinction can be drawn between *some* of the sorts of examples given here. Ernst Gombrich says that (contrary to what is said in the example above) 'normally the table looks the shape it is. If it is rectangular, it looks rectangular, and we are perfectly aware of its shape, rather than of its perspective appearance.' I am not going to give *the* answer to the question 'Are all the examples similar?', or even possible answers. I just want to make sure that you do not accept the list of examples unquestioningly, without thinking about them at all, but are prepared to connect them with the TV programme, and with my subsequent discussion.)●

Now suppose we had a philosopher called A who said the following:

A: You can't rely on your senses, or not on vision anyhow. They deceive you. They make you think that you are seeing something elliptical when you look at a penny, that your house is no bigger than a matchbox, that the table has obtuse and acute angles rather than right angles, that your body is behind the glass, that the tomato has white streaks on it, that the grass, heather or rocks on the distant hillside are blue; they make you think the straight stick in water is bent. The penny looks exactly like something elliptical, your house on the horizon looks exactly like something the size of a matchbox, and so on. No wonder we are constantly deceived.

Well, what do you think? Do you think we are constantly deceived? (Do you usually think your body is behind the glass, for instance? Have you frequently thought a shiny tomato had a streak of white paint on it?)●

ANSWER

Not *constantly*. We often aren't deceived at all.
Now the question is, *why* are we not deceived on the sorts of occasions A has described? (Think about checking up.)●

DISCUSSION

One possible (and very good) answer is that we cross-check our first sight by touch, or by doing tests, or by waiting and seeing. Remember the Müller–Lyer lines? *At first sight* (and without due warning from me) you may have been deceived into thinking that they were unequal lengths, but a quick test with a couple of rulers makes it clear that they aren't. If you had actual arrows which looked like the Müller–Lyer lines you could quickly feel that they were the same length.

Another possible (and very good) answer consists in *denying* something A said. If you haven't thought of it already, could you try to think of it now? Make sure it *is* an answer; it should begin, 'We are often not deceived because . . .' (Clue: *Does* e.g. the rectangular table look *exactly* like something with two acute angles and two obtuse angles, i.e. like something that *isn't* rectangular?)●

ANSWER

We are not deceived because it is *not true* that the penny looks exactly like something elliptical; not true that the house on the horizon looks exactly like something the size of a matchbox; not true that the rectangular table looks anything other than rectangular and so on. The penny does not look elliptical; it looks like a round thing seen from an angle. My house on the horizon looks like a large thing a long way off. The table looks like a rectangle seen from an angle and so on.

What do you think about the straight stick in water?●

DISCUSSION

The stick in water does not look *exactly* like an ordinary bent stick. It looks exactly like a stick in water. I can see the glass and the water, and we all know what happens when you put straight sticks in water. But I think we could agree with A that it does look bent. It seems foolish to deny it.

I must tell you that some philosophers recklessly *did* deny it, and went so far as to insist that the stick in water does not even look bent, but simply looks like a straight stick in water. There is a famous and very funny story associated with one such philosopher. He was lecturing on this topic and someone brought in a glass of water with a stick in it and challenged him. 'Do you mean to say,' he said, 'that this stick doesn't look bent!?' And the philosopher said firmly that no, it didn't look bent, it looked like a straight stick in water. And then they took the stick out of the water and it *was* bent.

That philosopher, and others like him, were over-reacting. This is quite an easy thing to do. Suppose someone has put forward the extreme view that we are constantly deceived because things constantly look other than they are (the round penny looks elliptical, the large house looks no bigger than a matchbox, the straight stick looks bent). This extreme view is obviously wrong and, rushing to deny it and assert common sense, it is quite easy to over-react and go to the opposite extreme. And then one winds up in the absurd position of saying things never look other than they are and so we are never deceived (the round penny never looks elliptical, the large house never looks no bigger than a match-box, the straight stick never looks bent). And *that* extreme view is wrong too.

As so often happens, the truth is somewhere in between. Sometimes, when we rely on what we see, we make mistakes about how things are. But we don't make many mistakes; in part because we do not, when 'relying on what we see', rely on a sole glance which isolates one feature. It is *possible* that *if* we were static creatures, that is, never moved, and *if* we did not have binocular vision and *if* the world were organized by a malicious demon who continually arranged distorted rooms and Müller–Lyer lines around us – *if* things were that way, then perhaps we would be wrong quite often. Perhaps it would be reasonable to doubt the reliability of our eyes. But things are *not* that way, and we are *not* often deceived.

But suppose the sceptic says this: 'When I said "Our senses are deceptive", I didn't mean that we often made mistakes because our senses deceive us. I meant that it is as if they *tried* to deceive us but we were too clever for them. That is, they tell us lies which we very cleverly *interpret* in such a way as to get at the *truth*. But *they* don't tell us the truth; they don't show us things as they really are.'

1.5   DO OUR SENSES DO THEIR PROPER JOB?

If the sceptic says that, the first thing we ask him, as usual, is 'What are your grounds for saying that our senses do not show us things as they really are?' What would you think if he said this:

The sceptic: When I look at myself in the mirror, my body appears to be some distance behind the glass. But it is really in front of the glass, so the perception is not veridical (truth-telling) but delusive.

He is not pretending to do more than give us an example of our senses telling us lies. But what do you think of the example?

If you do not immediately object to it, what do you think of this picture?

It gives one quite a jolt, doesn't it? If you were that man, i.e. if you looked into a mirror and saw the back of your own head, what would you think?

I would wonder whether I really was looking in a mirror in front of me, and I'd reach out and feel and tilt it to see how it reflected bits of the room around me. I'd wonder whether it was a mirror at all – perhaps there was a movie camera behind me filming the back of my head and somehow projecting this film onto a screen in front of me which had been made to look like a mirror. If someone, somehow, managed to convince me that I was looking in a perfectly ordinary mirror and that no tricks were involved, I could only conclude that I was undergoing some sort of hallucination, that is, that my eyes were not doing their proper job.

But would this be simply because my eyes *made it look as though my body were behind this glass?* Of course not. It would be because my eyes made it look as though I was seeing a reflection that just couldn't be there in an ordinary mirror.

Having thought about how disconcerting it would be to see a reflection of the back of one's head, think how disconcerting it would be to see no reflection at all.

93

And *now* what do you say to this:

A: When I look at myself in the mirror, my body appears to be some distance behind the glass. But it is really in front of the glass, so the perception is not veridical (truth-telling) but delusive. My senses are not doing their proper job. They are telling me lies.

Do you agree?●

SPECIMEN ANSWER

In showing me a reflection in a mirror at (presumably) the correct apparent distance behind the glass (correct according to the laws of refraction and perspective) my senses *are* doing their proper job. If they showed me no reflection at all *then* they would not be doing their proper job.

I mentioned earlier that mirages could be photographed, as though this were an important point. I think it is an important point in this context because, as we say, 'the camera does not lie'. Cameras faithfully record not only mirages, but reflections in mirrors, round pennies looking elliptical, the stick in water looking bent, the shine on the tomato, my house on the horizon as a small box, and so on. When my eyes are doing their proper job, they do the *same*.

If you are tempted to think of any of these examples as cases where my eyes somehow do *not* do their proper job, ask yourself the question, 'What would it be like if they *did* do their ⌜proper⌝ job?' Would we be seeing things as they really are if we never saw reflections in ⌜mirrors⌝? Can you see why I have put scare quotes around 'mirrors' in that question?●

DISCUSSION

What would a ⌜mirror⌝ be if it didn't reflect things? And if it (really) reflected things how could we be seeing things as they really are if reflections were not amongst the things we saw?

Would we be seeing things as they really are if we never saw the ⌜shine⌝ on a tomato but saw it as uniformly red?●

DISCUSSION

Well, is the tomato really shiny or isn't it? If it really is shiny then, *if* we are seeing things as they really are, we will see that it is shiny.

Would we be seeing things as they really are if we saw the penny as round from whatever angle we looked?●

DISCUSSION

What *does* look round from whatever angle we look?●

ANSWER

A sphere. Would our eyes be doing their proper job if they told us that a penny was a sphere? Obviously not. Should our eyes be doing something different with the sphere, then? It's hard to imagine what it could be. So our eyes would *not* be doing their proper job if they showed us the penny as round from whatever angle we looked. Would our eyes be doing their proper job if things always looked the same size, no matter how close or far away we were? This, I find, is a very hard one to imagine at all. For the moment let me raise a related question.

94

The sceptic's implication seems to be that when I look at my house on the far distant horizon and it looks no bigger than a matchbox, I am not seeing it as its *right* size. And the further implication is that something *does* count as seeing my house as its right size. My 'related question' is – *when* do I see things as the size they are? How close do I have to get to my house before I see it as its right size? Of course I must not get too close. When my nose is pressed against the front door I can't see whether it is one storey or twenty storeys high. Not too far, not too close – what is *the* magical distance from which I see my house as its *real, right* size?

I would say that this is an unanswerable question – or else that the answer is 'practically any distance you like as long as you can still see the house'.

Comprehension questions on this section

Question 1

What grounds does the sceptic have for saying our senses (well, sight) do not do their proper job? Please write down a one-sentence answer.●

ANSWER

(a) A general answer would be: 'Illusions', or 'The existence of illusions.' (b) A specific answer would be: 'Illusions such as the round penny looking elliptical, or the body appearing to be some distance behind the mirror.'

Question 2

Do his grounds support his view that our senses do not do their proper job?●

SPECIMEN ANSWER

No. I argued that in the case of many so-called illusions our eyes *were* doing their proper job and that this could be made strikingly obvious by considering how crazy things would be if our eyes did *not* do the things the sceptic implied were wrong.

Question 3

Am I committed to saying our senses *always* do their proper job? (A rash generalization?) (Look at the answer to Question 2.)●

ANSWER

No. If you answered 'Yes', look back up at Question 2 and the specimen answer. I have not been arguing against 'Our senses (sometimes) do not do their proper job.' I have been arguing against 'When I look at a mirror my body appears to be behind the glass, and it isn't; *therefore* my senses sometimes do not do their proper job', or 'When I look at my house on the horizon I do not see it as its right size; *therefore* my senses sometimes do not do their proper job.'

I am committed to saying that our senses do their proper job on all those occasions on which the sceptic said they did *not*. I haven't said anything about whether they *always* do their proper job.

Question 4

Well, do they? What do you think? In earlier sections, have we mentioned examples which *would* support the view that our senses sometimes do not do their proper job?●

DISCUSSION

Yes, we have. The Müller–Lyer lines and the distorted room both seem to me to be cases where we do *not* see things as their right size. I think it would also be quite natural to describe the hallucination examples as cases of one's senses not doing their proper job. (One could quibble and say, 'But the hallucinogenic drugs don't affect my *eyes*. They affect my brain.' All right, but the net result is that I wind up seeing things as other than they are. And even if this is because of a malfunction in my brain rather than my eyes, I still don't need to put scare quotes around the word 'seeing'.)

2 REALITY

2.1 INTRODUCTION

In the first part of this unit I have been discussing the sceptic who denied that we perceived things as they really are, on grounds concerning certain illusions. In maintaining that things seemed to us to be thus and so, whereas *really* they were otherwise (the penny seemed to us to be elliptical, but is really round, etc.), he was drawing one of the oldest and most problematic distinctions in philosophy: the distinction between appearance and reality. Whether we do perceive things *'as* they really are' is a question that, of course, must get involved with *how* things really are, that is, with reality. I have already criticized some of the things the sceptic says about appearance and seeming. Now I shall say something about Reality.

Despite that grand capital letter you will not be surprised to hear that I do not manage to cover all reality; I discuss only shape, colour, and a couple of aspects of what scientists can tell us about how things really are.

2.2 REAL SHAPE

What do you think of the following argument? 'From different angles, the coin will appear a variety of different shapes; only one of them is the shape it really is, so it follows that only occasionally does the coin present a true (veridical) appearance but that mostly it presents a delusive one; or that occasionally we see it as it really is, but mostly we don't.'

Do you accept this conclusion? If you *don't,* can you put your finger on the bit or bits of the argument that you do not agree with? If you *do* accept it, or are not sure whether you do or do not, look at this one: 'From different distances the house will appear a variety of sizes; only one of them is the size it really is, so it follows that only occasionally does the house present a veridical appearance but that mostly it presents a delusive one; or that occasionally we see it as its real size, but mostly we don't.'

Now I hope that you will *not* accept the conclusion of this second argument and I hope you will agree with me about what is wrong with it. The bit I disagree with (and have disagreed with before on page 95) is the assumption that there is some special point at which we see the real size of the house. This is a fatally muddling way to describe what happens. There are some points at which it is quite impossible to see what size the house is (too far away, too close up) and many other points at which one can see very well that it is, for instance, two storeys high but that the storeys are not particularly high ones. And at those *many* points we see it as its right size.

Similarly I would maintain that the conclusion of the first argument is wrong, and that what is wrong with the argument is the premise that at some special point we see the real shape of the coin, or that only occasionally does it present a veridical appearance.

'But,' someone says, 'how can you deny that at some special point we see the real shape of the coin? You can't deny that there is at least one position from which it looks round, that is, the shape it really is.'

Well, yes, it really is round. But it really is flat too, and it really is about 1/16th of an inch thick. If someone says that we see the ⌜real⌝ shape when we see the coin head on and it looks round, shouldn't he say that we also see the ⌜real⌝ shape when we look at it truly side on, and see that it is 1/16th of an inch thick and flat top and bottom?

A coin is a *three*-dimensional object. When you describe the shape of a three-dimensional object by saying that it's round then *either* you mean it's a sphere *or* you have not yet given a full description of its shape. If an object is so cunningly hidden that I can only see one of its surfaces I cannot see what shape it is, though I may see that the shape of that *surface* is, say, round.

Do we ever see the real shape of a three-dimensional object? You *might* want to say 'No'. You *might* want to say, 'The only way you could ⌜see⌝ the real shape of a three-dimensional object would be if you had millions of eyes on tentacles so that you could look at the object from all the possible angles, simultaneously. That would be comparable to feeling the real shape of a three-dimensional object, which you can do if it is small enough for you to get both hands all round it. That's the only thing that would count as ⌜really seeing⌝ the real shape. And that is not how it is with us, so we never ⌜really see⌝ the real shape.'

I think that is a pointless thing to say. Why go to all the trouble of inventing a special sense of 'really see' in order to deny that in that special sense we really see? If we are being sensible then we say, 'Of course we can see the real shape of a three-dimensional object. You look at the penny on the table and you can see that it's round and flat on top and about 1/16th of an inch thick and you can see from the way it's lying on the table that it must have a flat bottom.' If we can see what its shape (really) is, that amounts to seeing its real shape.

Summary of this bit: I have just tried to show that what makes the argument on page 97 about shape plausible is that we can quite easily *think* that there are just one or two special points at which we do see the real shape, namely when it looks *round*. The argument manages to sound plausible because 'The penny really is round' or 'The table really is rectangular' *sound* like straightforwardly true remarks, and there are indeed just a few special points at which the perspectival appearance of the penny is a disc, or of the table a rectangle. So it is quite easy to be tricked into thinking that it is only when I see the penny or the table from e.g. directly above or below that I see what its shape really is.

But this is not a trick we should fall for *once* we realize that describing a three-dimensional thing as round or rectangular is *not* giving a complete description of its real shape. Suppose I know that the table is rectangular – do I know its real shape? Well, does it have legs, and if so how many, or is it a block with holes carved in it? Until I know, I don't know what shape it is, that is, I don't know its real shape, *despite* knowing that it is rectangular. If I want to find out its real shape, I look at it from several angles, peer underneath and so on. And then I know what its shape really is.

I don't know why we pretend to give a name to the real shape of such objects as coins and tables, saying, 'The coin really is round', 'The table really is rectangular', when really they are no such thing. Their plane (flat) surfaces are round or rectangular or elliptical or triangular, and perhaps it is primarily objects with plane surfaces that get described this way – I don't know; I should like the views of an expert in linguistics.

But we don't have to be experts to see that we do not even *pretend* to give a name to the real shapes of most objects; faced with most three-dimensional objects we wouldn't know how to set about answering the question, 'What is its real shape?' What is the real shape of – my car, my house, my lawn-mower, that chestnut tree? I can't say, but that's *not* because I don't know what shape each one really is. I know how to draw the distinction between my seeing these things as they really are and their appearing different to me – 'From this angle my car looks the same shape as a Volkswagen (though it isn't really)', 'I hadn't seen that your house has this bit out the back – it appears an almost perfect cube coming up the hill.' There are no words for the real shapes; usually there are no words for the apparent shapes either, and often we cannot say much about what shapes things appear beyond, 'Doesn't the lawn-mower look odd from this angle – almost as if the handle were twisted?' or 'If you look at the tree from here it looks as though it hasn't a trunk.'

As soon as we think in terms of these sorts of objects – objects with complex, lumpy, bitty shapes that don't have names – the argument on page 97 does not seem plausible at all. I walk round the car, or the house, or the lawn-mower or the tree – it does not sound at all plausible to say they appear a variety of shapes. I walk round them finding out what shape they are. It does not sound at all plausible to say that occasionally they present a true appearance but that mostly they don't. There are a *few* positions from which it is very hard to see what the real shape of such things is – too close, too far away, from just one very odd angle – but by and large we can walk all round a car, a house, a lawn-mower, a tree, get above them and look down from all sides, and view them from ever so many different angles – and from nearly all sides and angles they look just the shape they really are. And we can see what shape they really are.

The great philosopher Wittgenstein (1889–1951) identified 'A main cause of philosophical disease – a one-sided diet: one nourishes one's thinking with only one kind of example.' If we always think in terms of one kind of example – objects with plane surfaces whose shapes have a name – we can easily go quite wrong about real shape, and hence wrong about the distinction between real and apparent shape. It is wrong to say, 'The penny appears to be an ellipse, but it really is round.' The penny (*unless* viewed under exceptional and odd circumstances, when it presents an odd appearance so you can't tell what shape it is), appears to be round and flat; it is quite easy to see what its real shape is.

No-one wants to say, 'The car (the house, lawn-mower, tree) appears to be a . . . but is really . . .', so if we vary our philosophical diet with such examples, we find it easier to avoid mistakes. Such examples remind us that seeing something's shape is a complex business, because three-dimensional shape is a complex property. Though we may say that 'things look different from different points of view', this is not to say that mostly they do not look their real shape and occasionally do. They look different from different points of view because they are complex shapes. (Remember that a sphere is (one of?) the only thing(s) that one could say looked the same shape from whatever angle you viewed it.)

Even the further sorts of examples I have introduced are a bit one-sided. Think about objects that *move*. 'What,' as a philosopher once rhetorically asked, 'is the real shape of a cat?'

The real shape of a cat does not have a name; one might even say that the real shape of a cat (unless it is asleep) is constantly changing – but the distinction between real and apparent shape can still be drawn. Given a trick of light a cat might appear fat when it was thin; I will not be seeing its real shape if I see it in a distorting mirror, or through distorting spectacles; it might take me some time to notice that it was three-legged, or didn't have a tail, or was (what can only be described as) 'an odd shape', because it did not appear those ways, though it really was. So we can draw a distinction between seeing the cat as it really is, seeing its real shape, and not seeing the cat as it really is, but only as it appears. But it does not follow that we can answer the question 'What is the real shape of that cat?' either with a word ('round', 'rectangular'), or by pointing to just one of the pictures (as though one of them was the *true* appearance).

2.3   REAL COLOUR

A sceptic might try to argue that we do not, or only very rarely, ever see the real shape of a physical object, but he does not usually deny that there is such a thing as real shape. The shape of a thing is accessible to touch as well as sight. It is perceived by bats by radar. It is, one could argue, a property of objects which *must* be recognized, for, that square pegs won't go into round holes is a brute fact and how could a creature survive that could not somehow tell the difference between square and round?

But what goes for shape, and perhaps size and certain other properties, does not necessarily go for all the properties. It has been denied that there is such a thing as *real* colour, and, consequently, it has been denied that we ever see the real colour of a physical object.

Make sure you can see the difference between *this* criticism of our sight, and the other one about real shape; they are easily confused with each other.

The sceptic about our perception of shape says, 'Alas, alack, things *really are* certain shapes but we rarely or never, see their real shape. Our senses do a poor job.' It is unclear whether he thinks that there might be a creature who, fortunate in the possession of millions of eyes on tentacles, ⌐really⌐ could see the real shape; or whether he thinks that shape can be known only by touch. Indeed it is quite unclear on what grounds he is so sure that e.g. the penny really is round, but he *is* sure and his complaint is that things really are certain shapes but that we *don't* (or only rarely) perceive them as having those shapes, i.e. we don't perceive things as they really are.

The sceptic about our perception of colour says, 'Alas, alack, we perceive things as having certain colours but there is no such thing as real colour. Things really aren't coloured but we *do* perceive things as coloured, i.e. we don't perceive things as they really are.'

Now there are bad and good grounds for denying that things are really coloured and hence a silly and a sensible thing to mean by 'Colour is not real.' Before reading on, think a little about that sentence – 'Colour is not real.' If someone you respected said that, what sort of grounds would you expect him to give? What would you count (if anything) as supporting such a claim? I'm not about to answer that question. I want it to be something you have thought about before you read on.●

When do we see the real colour of something? Well, let's try to get to the answer by a process of elimination. Let's think about the things that can go wrong.

I go to a shop to buy a black frock for formal occasions. The one I buy looks black to me, and to the assistant in the shop, but when I get it home I find it is really a very dark blue. As anyone who has tried to buy matching gloves, scarves, socks and handkerchiefs knows, artificial light can be very deceptive. In the shop they all match; when you get them home they are not really the same colour after all.

On what grounds do we say that the frock is really dark blue rather than black? On what grounds do we say that the socks and handkerchief are really different colours (or different shades of the same colour) rather than the same colour?●

SPECIMEN ANSWER

We allow natural light, sunlight, to set the standard. The colour a thing looks in daylight is the colour it really is; the colour it looks in artificial light may or may not be its real colour.

The next question is – looks to whom? Suppose we have three people and a piece of paper in ordinary daylight. One of them says, 'It's in daylight and it looks white so it is white.' Another says, 'It's in daylight and it looks green so it is green.' The third reasons, 'It's in daylight and it looks yellow so it is yellow.' They can't all be right. Can you guess what has happened?●

SPECIMEN ANSWER

The story I tell is that the second person is wearing green-glass spectacles and the third has jaundice. It doesn't matter whether you told exactly the same story, as long as you said something about two of the people not having normal sight.

If the first person is the one with normal sight, and the other two are the ones without it, then the piece of paper really is white. The colour a thing looks in daylight *to someone with normal sight* is the colour it really is. We do not allow its real colour to be determined by how it looks to people wearing funny spectacles, or people who have jaundice or are colour-blind. (To them, geraniums and their leaves look the same colour; but we say they are really different colours.)

So far so good. But if that is how we determine what the real colour of something is, real colour begins to seem rather arbitrary. Can you identify *two* features which someone could argue were arbitrary?●

DISCUSSION

Someone could ask, 'Why should we make daylight set the standard? What is so special about daylight? Don't we just decide to *say* that how things appear in daylight is the colour they really are, and couldn't we just as well decide to say something else? So isn't is arbitrary?' So *one* feature which could be said to be arbitrary is our appeal to daylight. The second feature which seems arbitrary is the appeal to normal vision. For what is *normal* vision? Isn't it simply the vision that most human beings happen to have, that is, something determined by majority vote?

Neither of these factors is quite as arbitrary as I have made out. Can you think of an objection? (In terms of maximum discrimination, that is spotting the most differences.)●

SPECIMEN ANSWER

We can argue like this: people with normal vision can discriminate more colours than can people who are colour-blind. They can sort red things and green things into separate piles. Either they all, consistently and constantly, hallucinate a difference (which would cry out for explanation) or there really is a difference there which the colour-blind person cannot spot. Similarly, daylight provides conditions of maximum discrimination. Two frocks which both look black in artificial light look different in daylight; one dark blue and the other black. So either daylight quite inexplicably causes us all to hallucinate a difference, or there really is a difference there. (In neither case is hallucination the only alternative, but any others are equally odd, and call for explanation.)

We could still say, 'But why insist on calling the colour it looks in daylight the *real* colour? Why shouldn't we say of some frocks that they *are* black but look blue in daylight? There's absolutely no reason not to.'

Well, there is *one* reason, given the way things are. We can predict of certain dark blue frocks that they will look black in artificial light; but we cannot predict of the frocks that look black in artificial light which will look black and which blue in daylight. That is, once you have described something as dark blue (the colour it looks in daylight) you have already told everyone familiar with artificial light that the thing may look black under it. Whereas if you describe the thing as black (the colour it looked under artificial light) none of us would know whether it will look black or blue in daylight.

There is an odd sort of semi-precious stone which looks (I think) greenish in daylight and purple in artificial light. In this case we do not insist on calling the colour it looks in daylight the *real* colour, and I think this is because saying it was green would not give anyone a *hint* as to what it would look like in artificial light. Nor do we say that purple is its real colour. The only thing to say about its real colour is what I said when I first described it – it looks greenish in daylight and purple in artificial light.

So, as things are, there is some reason to opt for people with normal vision (maximum discrimination) and daylight (condition of maximum discrimination). But we still seem to have some sort of problem. If the colour a thing looks in daylight to someone with normal vision is the colour it really is, what would be the case if normal vision were different?

As things are, most of us can distinguish between red and green. But what if most (or all) of us found that they looked the same? That is, what if most (or all) of us were what we *now* call colour-blind?

Then geraniums and their leaves, blood and grass, pillar boxes and trees would all be, really, the same colour (though they might be different shades of the same colour).

Do you find that a startling conclusion? I think it is, and am not surprised that people want to express it by saying, 'Colour is subjective', or 'Colour is not real.' But let us look *very* carefully at what is meant by saying either of those two things.

Remember my third rather odd definition of 'subjective definition' as 'a judgement in which the speaker says something about himself as a thinking thing, or as a person' (Unit 14, page 57). I said that it came from an old use of 'subjective', according to which it means *'relating* to a thinking subject'. The important word there is 'relating'.

Colour properties are *relational*. 'Pillar boxes are red' looks, grammatically, as though it says something simply about pillar boxes (as 'A101 is difficult' looks, grammatically, as though it says something simply about A101). But, as we realize when we think about it carefully, 'Pillar boxes are red' (like 'A101 is difficult') says something implicitly about people and their *relation* to pillar boxes (or A101). 'Pillar boxes are red' amounts to 'Pillar boxes are such that they look red to people with normal vision in daylight', which does not say something simply about pillar boxes, but also about people and how they are related to pillar boxes.

Given that 'Pillar boxes are red' is not only about pillar boxes but also about people, it should not be surprising that by changing *either* the pillar boxes, *or* the people, we could change the truth of 'Pillar boxes are red.' If the pillar boxes are changed (e.g. painted) then one factor has changed, so 'Pillar boxes are red' might cease to be true. And if *people* changed (e.g. if our eyes became different), then the other factor has changed and, once again 'Pillar boxes are red' might cease to be true. It might become true that pillar boxes, like geraniums and their leaves and grass, were all green.

If you find that hard to follow, try the parallel with 'A101 is difficult.' It says something implicitly about people; it amounts to (something like) 'A101 is such that the average OU student does, or would, find it difficult.' By changing either the course, or the people, we could change the truth of 'A101 is difficult.' We could change the course (e.g. by dropping the philosophy units!), and then 'A101 is difficult' might cease to be true. And if people changed – for example if the national average IQ went up overnight, or, more mundanely, if everyone started doing preparatory courses, so that nearly everyone sailed through A101 – then, in that case, 'A101 is difficult' would cease to be true. Note that I could express the last point by saying: although A101 hadn't changed at all, it might cease to be difficult and become easy. That sounds paradoxical, but not when you remember that being easy or difficult is not a simple property of A101, but a relation holding between A101 and the people who do it.

Given that colour properties are relational, and, moreover, related to *us*, as conscious, or thinking things, they are subjective in the sense of 'relating to a thinking subject'. And now we can understand what could be sensibly meant by saying colours are not real. To think that there is something particularly superior about our eyes, something peculiarly perfect about the normality of our normal vision, which guarantees that, for instance, all red things have something in common, a real property inherent in the objects,[1] which creatures with different sense-organs might learn about by different means – to think that is to make a complete mistake. To think because *our* eyes see pillar boxes and grass as different, and pillar boxes and blood are similar, that there are real differences and similarities there, which *any* creature should know about if it is to know how things really are – that is to make a mistake.

But of course that does *not* mean that colours are hallucinatory, or that we just imagine them or make them up. It does not mean that anyone's opinion goes on whether someone's frock is dark blue or black, or whether a tomato is uniformly red or has a white streak of paint on it, or whether a piece of paper is white or green. We can draw a distinction between seeing things as they really are, seeing what colours they really are, and not seeing them as they really are, but only as they appear. When we claim that something is black, or green, or striped we are making a claim about objective reality and there is a genuine question about whether one is right or wrong. The frock appeared black but it is really, yes really, dark blue; the paper appeared green but is really white; the tomato appeared to have a stripe, but is really a uniform red, and so on.

To coin a phrase, there is both more and less to reality than meets the eye; and that thought leads us to the next section.

2.4   ON NOT BEING DAZZLED BY SCIENCE ABOUT REAL QUALITIES

Polished table tops and tomatoes are smooth, unlike sandpaper and tables made out of undressed wood. They look smooth and feel smooth. What would you say to someone who insisted that they weren't really smooth? Surely he must be wrong. But suppose he pointed out that under a microscope the polished table top is revealed to be pitted and cratered like the surface of the moon and not smooth at all! What do we say then?

---

[1] This footnote is intended *only* for people who know some physics and have been bursting to mention light waves. Many people – including, I might say, most philosophers who write on this subject – assume that there is a one-to-one correlation between different colours and different wavelengths. It is quite natural to move from this assumption to the idea that there *is* a real property inherent in any red object, namely that-in-virtue-of-which-it-reflects wavelengths of such and such a length, and absorbs the others; that this *is* a property which our eyes are very clever at spotting, since we do see all the colours on the colour spectrum, and that it *is* a property which any creature should know about if it is to know how things really are: even if it didn't have eyes to spot the different wavelengths, it should be able to spot them somehow, because they really are there. I wish I could go into this at length, but space permits only the following. If you think of our eyes as instruments for spotting wavelengths, they are very bad at it. (i) Compare how good our ears are at detecting different sound waves, with how bad our eyes are at detecting different wavelengths. We can distinguish a mixture of sound waves – if four instruments all play a note at the same time we can often distinguish all four sounds within the complex sound of the chord. But although (so-called) white light does consist of a mixture of all the wavelengths in the colour spectrum we do not see it as, as it were, a symphony of colour. This is not just a peculiarity of white. (ii) *Some* things we see as red are reflecting (by and large) just those waves that are called red-making rays. *But*, all sorts of *different* mixtures of wavelengths will also make us see red – a red that looks just the same as that in the thing reflecting pure light. And the same is true of all the spectral colours. (iii) Dozens of colours we see aren't on the colour spectrum – white, black, grey, all the pastels, maroon, olive, crimson, damson, all the browns – and our *eyes* don't tell us that they are mixed and that the so-called spectral colours are pure. (iv) We see red and purple as similar, as easily shading into each other, but red and green as entirely different; but red and purple are at opposite ends of the spectrum, less close than red and green. Anyone dedicated to pursuing this very difficult topic could try reading *Perception: Facts and Theories*, by C. W. K. Mundle, Oxford University Press, London, 1971.

Even worse, what do we say to someone like Eddington, whom Ossie Hanfling quoted in Units 2B and 9?[1] Eddington said that science has shown that ordinary solid objects like tables and planks and blocks of marble are not really solid. He pointed out that according to modern physics all matter consists of tiny electrical charges, very thinly spaced and in constant motion. Ossie Hanfling said that we shouldn't blindly accept that science-has-shown that solid things aren't really solid – but how can we deny it, without trying to tell the physicists that we know more about the matter than they do?

One philosopher replied to Eddington like this:

> What are we to understand by 'solidity'? Unless we do understand it we cannot understand what the denial of solidity in the plank amounts to. But we can understand 'solidity' *only* if we can truly say that the plank is solid. For 'solid' just is the word we use to describe a certain respect in which a plank of wood resembles a block of marble, a piece of paper and a cricket ball, and in which each of these differs from a sponge, from the interior of a soap-bubble, and from the holes in a net . . . *If* the plank appears to be solid, but is really non-solid, what does 'solid' mean? If 'solid' has no assignable meaning, then 'non-solid' is also without sense. If the plank is non-solid, then where can we find an example to show us what 'solid' means? (L. Susan Stebbing, *Philosophy and the Physicists*)[2]

What do you think of that reply?●

I hope you have not dismissed Stebbing's argument by saying, 'Oh, it's just about words.' Words *matter*. If we cannot understand what Eddington's words mean, we cannot understand what he says, and hence we don't know whether what he says is true or false.

What I object to in Stebbing's reply (as it stands here, in isolation) is that it suggests that we all know perfectly well what solidity is – it is that respect in which a plank resembles a block of marble and differs from a sponge or a block of foam rubber – and there is *nothing* for the physicists to tell us about it. Whereas it seems absurd to deny that the physicists told us something pretty interesting. What was it they told us?

Well, the naive way to think of 'that respect in which a plank resembles a block of marble' is to picture the plank and the marble as made up of teeny billiard-ball-type atoms, packed together so closely that there is no room between any two for another one. And physics *has* shown that that picture is wrong. But Eddington infers from this that the plank and block of marble are not solid and this is very misleading, for it suggests that there is no difference between a plank and a sponge, no difference between a block of marble and a block of foam rubber. All this time I have been thinking there *was* a difference; has science shown I was wrong?

No. That, of course, physics has *not* shown. On the contrary, physics provides us with a unified account of the difference, an account, moreover, that explains why it is that if you get the foam-rubber table cold enough it *will* be solid and, behaving like a glass table, will shatter if you hit it with a hammer.

It's not that science has shown that planks and tables are not solid. Science has given us a better understanding of what solidity (that respect in which planks resemble tables and differ from clouds and blocks of rubber) *is*. It has given us a better understanding of reality.

Now go through for yourself the same sort of argument to knock down the person who says that the microscope reveals that polished table tops are not really smooth.●

---

[1] Page 25.
[2] Penguin, Harmondsworth, 1944.

SPECIMEN ANSWER

If I found what was revealed by the microscope startling, I must have had a false picture about what was involved in something's being smooth. Perhaps I did think vaguely that, even to the smallest insect around, the polished table top and the tomato must present uniform surfaces. If I was thinking that way, then the microscope reveals that it was the wrong way. But does the microscope reveal that I was wrong in thinking there was a difference between the polished table top and the tomato on the one hand, and sandpaper and a table top of undressed wood on the other? That the former are not really smooth, the way they appear, but really rough, like the others?

No. The microscope reveals no such thing. On the contrary, the microscope reveals the relative difference between the smooth and the rough. If the table top looks corrugated under the microscope, the sandpaper looks like a plain littered with hugh boulders; if silk looks like a doormat, the doormat looks like a forest of thick trees.

Figure 6   Surface of sandpaper magnified about 1,500 times

So do we perceive the world as it really is? Well, we perceive a difference between planks and sponges, and there really is a difference. We perceive a difference between polished table tops and sandpaper, and there really is a difference. So far so good. There are all sorts of differences that we *don't* perceive too (as science has shown), and if we assumed that because we didn't perceive them they weren't really there we really would be being naive.

3 SENSE-DATA

3.1 INTRODUCTION

It is time we got back to the sceptic. Please would you turn back and re-read the introductory dialogue on page 85. B finishes up saying, 'Why shouldn't I rely on my senses?' and in the first half of the unit we have been considering various attempts the sceptic can make to answer this question of B's, trying to cast doubt on the reliability of our senses and, hence, on our knowledge of the world about us. He (the sceptic) tried to show that the ordinary justification we give of statements about the external world, in terms of what we can see and touch and hear and so on, was *never* good enough, because it involved relying on our senses.

You may feel that we have done enough on the sceptic, and find yourself becoming impatient with some of the questions raised in what follows. If so, I'm sorry, but I cannot do anything more than quote the comment of one of the developmental-testing students at the end of the philosophy block: 'If one does a course such as A101 to increase one's knowledge, I suppose it makes good sense to begin by discussing knowledge and to answer the question – can we have real knowledge of anything?'

We explore that question when we take the sceptic seriously and argue against him. Much of the value lies in the exploration itself, but this *is* something that requires patience.

If we argue against him the way we have been doing in the preceding sections of this unit, we learn a great deal about what 'relying on our senses' involves. We notice what a complex process the perception of shape and size is; we learn to think again about the truth of such statements as 'the penny is round'; we learn (if we saw the TV programme on perception) that there are different senses of the word 'appear'; we learn that though colour and shape are both perceptible properties, colour is a different sort of property, a relational property, and in one sense, subjective. And our understanding of appearance, and reality, and our perception of them, is greatly increased. That is why I said, at the end of the first philosophy unit, that one learns a lot from trying to show where the sceptic goes wrong.

But there is another way of reacting to the sceptic's arguments concerning the reliability of our senses and that is to seek certainty in perception elsewhere. A philosopher who does this *concedes* that the ordinary justification we give for our statements about the external world is not good enough, being convinced by the arguments concerning illusions and hallucinations, and retreats to a position where he tries to find a better justification.

Think back to Descartes and the statements that philosophers thought might be candidates for Cartesian truths. Amongst them I mentioned 'statements of immediate experience such as "I *seem* to see a white page in front of me" (nothing reckless and dubitable about actually seeing one)'.[1] I could also say, 'I see something whose shape has two acute angles and two obtuse angles', or 'I see the appearance of something white and square.' And all these statements are taken as claiming *not* that I see the white page, but that I see something *else* – a sense-datum.

The idea generalized from this sort of example – that I do not see, touch, smell, hear, or taste physical objects, but something else, sense-data – this idea seems to have both plausibility and all sorts of advantages.

One apparent advantage is the one just mentioned – certainty. However hard I fight back against the sceptic concerning the reliability of our senses, I have to admit that they sometimes let me down (cf. pp. 85–88). They are certainly not

[1] Unit 13, page 38 above.

106

infallible. But in the sense-data statements I do seem to find Cartesian indubitability. The sceptic can push me back further and further – yes, I might be wrong about its being a page; perhaps it's not paper but a patch of light; perhaps it's not white, perhaps it's not squarish; perhaps there's no *it* out there at all and I'm hallucinating – but one thing I'm *sure* about and that is that I'm certainly seeing something that has the look of a white page in front of me. He can't shake me on *that*.

A second apparent advantage which a number of philosophers saw in the idea was that it seemed to contribute something important to the theory of perception. We do not need a sophisticated physiological theory to recognize that perception is a causal process. Long before anything was known about the *brain* (Aristotle, over 2,000 years ago, thought that the centre of the perceptual system was to be found in the heart), it was taken to be obvious that we see because objects in the world somehow affect our eyes; we hear because our ears are affected, and, in general, what happens in perception is that the object perceived *causes* something to happen in one's body.

In one's body? Well, yes, but philosophers following Descartes wanted to say that, more importantly, something happened in one's *mind*. According to this line of thought we are conscious of sense-experiences, or sensations, when we perceive, and this is something extra and important. Extra, because without it, we don't perceive, no matter what is caused to happen in our body – I do not perceive the striking of the clock when I am asleep, or the softness and coolness of the sheets, though my body is presumably affected in the same way as when I am awake; if I do not register my cheque book on the mantelpiece I do not perceive it, even if it is 'staring me in the face' and affecting my eyes in the very same way it does when I notice it, am conscious of my visual experiences and do perceive it. So sense-experiences, or sensations, or sense-data seem to be necessary to perception and hence important, as part of the causal story of what happens when we perceive.

They are also important because they seem to be sufficient, i.e. we don't always need anything to happen in our body in order to perceive. What happens, after all, when I hallucinate? When Macbeth hallucinates his dagger there is no dagger affecting his eyes. But he is seeing *something* – sense-data.

So here, apparently, is a third great advantage in the introduction of sense-data – it allows one to give a uniform account of what happens in both ordinary perception and hallucination. There *is* something common to both and what it is is the perception of sense-data.

This can lead to yet another, fourth advantage. How does Macbeth find out he is hallucinating? He says, 'Come let me clutch thee:/I have thee not and yet I see thee still.' He double-checks, in this case with the sense of touch. Similarly, when we see the bent stick, we feel it to find out whether it is bent. We also double-check things like shapes by viewing things from many angles. Earlier in the unit we came to realize that perceiving, for example, shape, was a complex process – and it looks as though the process can now be described. Working from the basic data, the sense-data, which are known directly, we build up by inference a picture or view of the world around us. Working, for example, from all the elliptical sense-data, we build up our picture of the round penny. Working from all the round red patches with white stripes, we build up our picture of the shiny tomato.

Finally, and fifthly, some philosophers thought that here was the point at which we could go back and rebut the sceptic. From a solid basis of Cartesian indubitability (sense-data statements) we could build up to making claims about the external world, giving these claims not the ordinary justification, in terms of seeing and touching physical objects, but a better justification, in terms of inferences from sense-data statements.

Before reading on, please state the five alleged advantages in introducing sense-data. (No more than one sentence per advantage.)●

ANSWER

The alleged advantages in introducing sense-data are that (i) sense-data statements give one a set of Cartesian truths and hence certainty, (ii) sense-data enable one to account for the obvious truth that perception is a causal process, (iii) they enable one to account for what is common to perception and hallucination, (iv) they enable one to describe the complex process of perception as proceeding by inference from basic given data and (v) sense-data statements enable one to rebut the sceptic by providing a better justification than the ordinary one for our statements about the external world.

The last alleged advantage was not one that all philosophers saw in the idea of sense-data. On the contrary, some philosophers realized that, far from enabling one to come back at the sceptic, the idea that we always perceive sense-data delivers us right into his grip.

For consider what an extraordinary position the idea gets us into. I aim to make a remark about the world around me – the trees outside the window, the chair I am sitting on, the page in front of me – and all these remarks are purely about *myself*, about my own personal, private sense-experiences. (The remarks are all subjective in the third sense I gave in the last unit.) But what I wanted to do was make an objective remark, a remark that was not just true for me, but more generally true; a remark about the world around me, which everyone else can perceive, which is not dependent on my existence, but would exist whether I perceived it or not. But how do I get there? It seems that I have cut myself off entirely from this world, stranded myself behind what the philosopher Jonathan Bennett has sarcastically nicknamed 'the veil of perception'. Through this veil I do not even perceive the external world darkly or dimly. I don't perceive it at *all*. I only perceive the sense-data. And how can I ever claim that the sense-data are caused by physical objects, and that they resemble physical objects, when never in my whole experience have I ever seen or touched a physical object to compare my sense-data with? The sceptic has me in the palm of his hand.

Where does he have you? Did you think the idea of sense-data sounded like a good one? It is an idea with a long history; it can be found in Aristotle and, in various forms, in the writings of some philosophers today. I think one reason why it has such a long history is that it is not of course a nonsensical or silly idea, but that, on the contrary, the reasons philosophers have had for introducing sense-data contained a lot of truths: about appearances, about perception, about knowledge, about conscious experience. But these truths have to be extracted, and separated from falsehood and muddles as wheat from chaff. If you did think the idea of sense-data sounded like a good one; if you let the last sentence in the Russell extract ('Let us give the name of "sense-data" to the things that are immediately known in sensation') pass unchallenged, then probably you have implicitly recognized some of the truths but still have something to learn about the falsehoods.

At this point I should remind you again of how very modest the aim of this unit is. Given a topic with a 2,000-year-old history, of *course* I am doing no more than scratching its surface, and it would be ludicrously presumptuous of me to claim that I had done justice to either the truths *or* the falsehoods contained in the writings of so many great philosophers on the topic. My modest aim is to send you back to the Russell extract with newly awakened eyes and to help you to see how the problem of perception connects with the sceptical position discussed in the first philosophy unit. If you can find places where I have gone wrong; if you can think of arguments for sense-data which are not subject to the criticisms I make, then the unit will have succeeded *beyond* its modest aim – you will have started to engage in philosophy. Take the arguments to summer school and try them out on people there – and you will have joined the ranks of philosophers, who argue together to get at the truth.

3.2   THE INTRODUCTION OF TECHNICAL TERMS

If we are going to sort the wheat from the chaff, the truths from the falsehoods, we have to be very suspicious of technical terms, which may (like the terms 'subjective judgement' or 'value judgement') be open to many interpretations. A statement containing one or more technical terms may have a deceptive grammatical simplicity which conceals a very complex view that contains both truths *and* falsehoods – truths when you interpret the terms *this* way, thinking of *these* examples, falsehoods when you interpret the terms *that* way, thinking of *those* examples.

So, bearing that in mind, let's bring the sceptic back in. Let's suppose that he now introduces a new argument to cast doubt on our knowledge of the world around us. He says, 'We don't have *direct* or *immediate* knowledge of physical objects in perception. Our knowledge, so-called, of the things about us – this table in front of us, the book on it, and so on – is not direct or immediate.'

What's the first thing we ask him? Please write your answer down: one question. (Or two – there is more than one good answer here.)●

DISCUSSION

Our *immediate* reaction should be one of caution and suspicion. I know what the difference is between an immediate and a delayed reaction; I know what someone is talking about when they say, 'He didn't know what it was immediately, but realized later that . . .' I know what it is to know something 'direct from the horse's mouth'. But 'direct and immediate knowledge' – that's not a term I'm used to. So it is probably being used in an odd way. So I had better be on my guard. So one thing I might ask him is, 'What do you mean, we don't have direct or immediate knowledge of physical objects?'

As I said in Unit 13,[1] though this may be a reasonable question, it is inclined to get the reply 'I meant what I said.' But often a good way of finding out what someone means by a claim is to ask him what his grounds for it are. So instead of asking him, 'What do you mean?' I could, perhaps more profitably, ask him, 'What are your grounds for saying that?'

If someone is using a term in an odd way, another way of finding out (a *bit* about) what he means by it is to ask him where or when or to what he thinks it applies. So the other thing I could ask him is, 'Oh really? What *do* we have ⌐direct or immediate knowledge⌐ of, then?'[2]

You should have got at least one of these, or something very like them. 'What do you mean by "direct and immediate knowledge"?', 'What are your grounds for saying that?', or 'What *do* we have ⌐ direct or immediate⌐ knowledge of, then?'

So now let's suppose that we both jumped on him when he made that claim: I asked him the second question and you asked him the third. He answers both of us simultaneously by saying, 'My grounds for that claim are that we do not really, or directly, *perceive* physical objects. What we directly or immediately perceive are ideas or sensations or sense-data, and it is of them that we have direct and immediate knowledge.'

What do we say now? (More than one good answer again.)●

DISCUSSION

Pretty obviously we should now direct our suspicions to the term 'directly and immediately perceive'. So, as before, one possible question is 'What do you

---

[1] Page 19.
[2] I use the scare quotes in my question because I am suspicious of this term. According to his reply I may drop the scare quotes *or* I may maintain that he ought to be using scare quotes too.

mean?' and, as before, it is probably more profitable to find out the answer to that question by asking a different one, namely 'What are your grounds . . .?' (Notice that if we are being careful we should separate 'What are your grounds for saying we do *not* really or directly perceive physical objects' from 'What are your grounds for saying we *do* directly or immediately perceive ideas or sensations or sense-data?') There is no point in asking, 'What *do* we directly or immediately perceive, then?' because on this occasion he has told us what he thinks his term applies to. According to him it applies to ideas, sensations or sense-data. Is there anything else we should be suspicious about and ask questions about?●

DISCUSSION

Remembering that 'perceive' is after all just shorthand for 'see, touch, hear, smell, or taste', I would be suspicious about his having said that we directly perceive ideas or sensations. I would think, 'I'm quite sure that, in general, I do *not* perceive ideas or sensations. I *have* them all right, but I don't see them or touch them or taste them, etc.' Of course, he has not yet told me what he means by '*directly* perceive', but if it means anything *like* ordinary 'perceive' then I suspect that, in this imaginary philosopher's mouth, 'idea' and 'sensation' are quasi-technical terms.

I always find it rather hard to be constantly on my guard about disguised technical terms (that is, ordinary terms such as 'idea' or 'sensation' being used in a technical way) because it is hard to remember, of an ordinary word, that it *is* being used technically. Since I want you to go on being suspicious about the terms the sceptic is employing, I am going to have him express his views using the *manifestly* technical term 'sense-data' (singular, 'sense-datum').

Now the thing to remember about technical terms is that they cannot, as it were, rise above their origins. They are no better than their mode of introduction. If a philosopher introduces a technical term into philosophical vocabulary by means of glossing over important differences, by basing his arguments on false premises or by relying on invalid arguments, by concentrating on certain examples and forgetting about others – if, in short, its introduction is a muddle – then the term itself will be a muddled term.

If it is a muddled term it might be possible to give several quite different definitions of it, all of which had their uses, but none of which was *correct*. (Does that sound like a familiar procedure? It should. It is what we did in the last unit with 'value judgement' and 'subjective judgement'.) But it is also possible that the term has such disreputable origins that we would do best by abandoning it entirely. The philosophers who introduced it might have been entirely wrong in thinking that we needed a technical term in this area at all.

In this part of the unit one philosopher, A, is going to be arguing for the introduction of the term 'sense-data' and trying to attach a clear meaning to it, and another philosopher, B, is going to be arguing that it is a term we neither need nor want. Don't bother about covering up the text. Read it straight through (but watch out for a couple of questions en route).

3.3   INTRODUCTION OF SENSE-DATA THROUGH ILLUSIONS

A: There's no difficulty about understanding the term 'sense-data'. Sense-data are what we perceive – the objects of perception.

B: We don't *need* another term for what we perceive – we perceive physical objects. We perceive tables, sticks, pennies, books, tomatoes, people, . . .

A (interrupting):   No we don't.

B: Huh?

A: We *don't* perceive tables and pennies and sticks and so on.

B: [The usual question.] What are your grounds for saying that? [No point in his asking, 'What *do* we perceive, then?' A gave his answer to that in the opening sentence.]

A: Well, let's take the straight stick in water. I'm going to use this example to argue that we do not see the stick, the physical object, but something else, a sense-datum. You remember about this example: when I look at a straight stick standing in a glass of water, what I see is bent. Now if I assume, with you, that I see the stick, we get a contradiction. The stick isn't bent, it's straight; what I see is bent; so if what I see is the stick, it is both bent and straight. Which is a contradiction. Obviously the assumption is wrong. *What I see* is not the stick, but something else – a sense-datum. [(Before B has a chance to reply, please would you try to do A's argument on other examples. Do the penny, the house on the horizon and the frock that looks different under artificial light. Then read on.]●

A (cont.):   Often, when I look at a penny, *what I see* is elliptical; the penny is round, so if I assume, with you, that I see the penny I get a contradiction – what I see is both round and elliptical. So the assumption is wrong. *What I see* is not the penny, but something else – an elliptical sense-datum. When I look at my house on the horizon, *what I see* is not much bigger than a matchbox. But my house is a great deal bigger than a matchbox; therefore: *what I see* is not my house but something else – a matchbox-sized sense-datum. When I look at my dark blue frock in artificial light *what I see* is black. So I don't see the frock, but something else – a black sense-datum. And when I look at myself in the mirror – *what I see* is in front of me. But of course I can't be in front of myself. So what I see is something else – a sense-datum.

What do you think of this argument of A's? Are you, for instance, convinced that there is, respectively, a bent stick, an elliptical penny, a matchbox sized house, a black frock, a mirror image? Which we see? Do you think all the cases are the same? What could B say in criticism of A? Try to think of an answer before reading on.●

B: I think the mirror-image case is different from the others. With the exception of the mirror-image case, the first premise in each of A's examples is false. When I look at a straight stick in water I do *not* see something bent; there is no bent stick there to be seen. I see the straight stick looking or appearing bent. When I look at a penny, I do not see something elliptical; there is nothing elliptical there to be seen. When I look at a penny, *what I see* is the penny; it may look or appear elliptical (in one sense of 'appear'); it may look like a thin brown line if I see it (note, *it*, not something else) side on, but even so the penny is what I see – the object of perception. Similarly I do *not* see anything matchbox-sized; there is nothing matchbox-sized there to be seen.

I do see a mirror image or a reflection all right, and it is, unlike my own body, in front of me. But what I see is not usually something like a reflection.

Summary: Are you clear about how this little bit of argument goes? A began by introducing the term 'sense-data' to mean 'objects of perception', that is, 'what we perceive'. B said we did not need such a term since we already had the term 'physical objects' to refer to the objects of perception. Physical objects are what we perceive. A denied this, and tried to use the so-called argument from illusion to show that e.g. when I look at a straight stick in water, *what I see* is bent, and

111

hence *what I see* is not the straight stick (the physical object) but something else. He cited several examples and concluded that, on at least many occasions, what I perceive are not physical objects; *so* we do need the term 'sense-data'. B attacked the premise that e.g. what I see is bent. He pointed out that there is no bent stick, elliptical penny, matchbox-sized house to be seen in the cases A cited; what I see in each case is the physical thing which may or may not *look* bent, elliptical, etc. So what I see, the object of perception, in all these cases, is a physical object. The exception is the mirror image. But seeing mirror images isn't what usually happens; we can't generalize (rashly) from the mirror-image case and say we *never* perceive physical objects, we *always* perceive sense-data.

So what follows about the term 'sense-data'? Well, what follows is that *this* way of introducing the term 'sense-data' hasn't worked. A tried to deny that we perceive physical objects and tried to introduce 'sense-data' as the term for what we do perceive. And B insisted that we *do* perceive physical objects, leaving the term 'sense-data' with nothing to do.

There are many ways in which this dialogue could go on. A might force B to admit that appearances were very important in perception. B could admit that how things appear to us is indeed a very important aspect of perception but sensibly refuse to admit that when I look at a table I see *two* things, a table *and* its appearance; or that I touch a table but see only its appearance (and so never see what I touch). If he could get A to see the absurdity of talking about appearances as though they were *things*, sense-data, then B and A could settle down to a profitable discussion of just what role how things appear to us plays in our acquiring knowledge of the external world. You will see (or will have seen) one such discussion in Television Programme 15.

But, in the next section, I imagine the dialogue continuing a different way, with no mention of appearances at all.

3.4   DIRECT AND INDIRECT PERCEPTION

One way the dialogue can continue is this:

A: Yes, of course I admit that in a sense you *do* perceive the penny (or the stick, frock, house, etc.). But, strictly speaking, you don't perceive the penny *directly*. What you *directly* perceive is a sense-datum.

B: That is a purely verbal manoeuvre. [Do you agree with B?]●

DISCUSSION

I certainly do. We are struggling to understand the justification for introducing the apparently unnecessary technical term 'sense-datum'; we *cannot* be led to an understanding of that technical term by the introduction of another technical term 'direct perception'. I'm not denying that this latter term can be given a sense. But at this stage of the imaginary dialogue it has not been given one and no amount of underlining and emphasis will perform the magic trick of making its new technical meaning crystal-clear.

Sometimes, instead of 'directly perceive', a philosopher may use 'directly aware of' or 'immediately perceive.' Sometimes he says that sense-data are what are immediately known or experienced, or directly known. The same remarks apply in all these cases:

Either (i) we *do* understand what is meant by these terms (in which case 'sense-data' turns out to be a term we don't really need) *or* (ii) we do *not* understand what is meant, in which case we are left grappling with two technical terms, neither of which has yet been explained.

Let's look at (i), the first alternative.

Giving it a sense

The terms 'direct perception', 'immediate perception' *might* be given a sense. Here is a quotation from a philosopher who is showing me what he means by (in this case) 'mediate' and 'immediate perception':

> . . . I grant we may, in one acceptation, be said to perceive sensible things mediately by sense: that is, when, from a frequently perceived connexion, the immediate perception of ideas by one sense *suggests* to the mind others, perhaps belonging to another sense, which are wont to be connected with them. For instance, when I hear a coach drive along the streets, immediately I perceive only the sound; but from the experience I have had that such a sound is connected with a coach, I am said to hear the coach. It is nevertheless evident that, in truth and strictness, nothing can be *heard* but *sound*; and the coach is not then properly perceived by sense, but suggested by experience.[1]

Figure 7   George Berkeley (1685–1753)

[1] From the first of the *Three Dialogues between Hylas and Philonous*, by George Berkeley (1685–1753).

113

Don't be put off by the rather archaic-sounding English in this passage. If you read it carefully it should be clear what Berkeley is saying. Make a note of the terms we are interested in and then answer the following questions.

1   What, according to Berkeley, happens when I, as we say, hear a coach? Do I have an immediate perception of it?●

ANSWER

No. According to Berkeley, '*im*mediately I perceive only the sound'. I know from past experience that the sound is the sort of sound that is caused by a coach, so I say, or it is said, that I hear the coach (which makes the sound).

2   Do I, in this case, perceive the coach at all, according to Berkeley?●

ANSWER

He grants, rather grudgingly, that I may be said to perceive it *mediately* but wishes to insist that this is not really *properly* perceiving the coach.

3   Putting Berkeley's points in terms of *direct* and *indirect* perception, when I hear a coach what, according to him, do I directly perceive and what do I indirectly perceive?●

ANSWER

When I hear a coach, what l ⌈directly perceive⌉[1] is (not the coach but) the sound caused by the coach. I perceive the coach ⌈indirectly⌉, via my ⌈direct perception⌉ of the sound it makes.

If someone introduces the technical terms 'direct perception' and 'indirect perception' in this way I think I can understand what he means. It is still not at all clear to me *why* he wants these terms, but he has given them a sense, and I think I know how to use them. According to the meaning he has given to the terms, we never ⌈directly perceive⌉ physical things by hearing; rather we always hear *sounds*.

But let us be careful. 'Perceive' covers not only hearing, but also smell, taste, sight and touch. Is it equally true of all these other four senses that we do not ⌈directly perceive⌉ (assuming we now understand this) physical objects, but something else? Think *carefully* about this one; it is a tricky question. Try to reproduce Berkeley's argument for each sense.●

DISCUSSION

I think that smelling and tasting are, in the relevant respect, similar to hearing. I can imagine Berkeley saying, 'When I smell fried onions, *im*mediately I perceive only the smell; but from the experience I have had that such a smell is connected with frying onions, I am said to smell the onions.' When I ⌈indirectly perceive⌉ fried onions, what I ⌈directly smell⌉ is (not the fried onions but) something caused by the fried onions, namely the oniony smell.

Tastes are perhaps a little different. Although it is easy to think of sounds and smells as things caused by, and separate from, physical things like coaches and onions, it is not so easy to think of tastes as being separate. But this example might do. When I eat the smoky-bacon-flavoured potato crisps I do not ⌈directly perceive⌉ the bacon. For all I know, I do not taste the bacon at all, for it may be that the flavour is synthetic. But what I do taste is the bacony taste and it is some*thing* that you could taste too.

[1] I'm putting scare quotes around these terms every time I use them in Berkeley's sense, just to remind us that I *am* using them in Berkeley's sense, which is a special one he has *given* to the terms.

114

So I think I would understand Berkeley if he said, 'We never hear, smell or taste physical things directly; rather, we always hear sounds, smell smells, and taste tastes.'

But I do *not* believe he could say, 'And we never see or touch physical things directly either; rather we always see . . . and touch . . .' What could he put in those blanks that made sense?

He could certainly say that *sometimes* we do not see physical objects ⌜directly⌝. Can you think of an example? (It should be a very familiar one by now.)●

ANSWER

When I, as we say, see myself in the mirror I do not see my body ⌜directly⌝. What I ⌜directly see⌝ is (not my body but) something caused by my body, namely, its reflection.

Another possible example would be the photographable mirage. When I , as we say, see the oasis on the horizon, what I ⌜directly see⌝ is (not the oasis, which is below the horizon but) something caused by the oasis, namely its mirage. A third possible example would be shadows. When I see you passing behind the curtain what I ⌜directly see⌝ is (not you but) something caused by you, namely your shadow.

So Berkeley could say that *sometimes* we do not see physical objects ⌜directly⌝. But he could *not* say, 'We never see physical objects directly; rather, we always see reflections, mirages, and shadows.' That is obviously completely false.

And finally, I do not think that we ever touch anything but things. I cannot imagine what would count as touching (not a thing but) something caused by a thing.

I am now going back to the dialogue between A and B. Remember, it begins like this (on page 112):

A: Yes, of course I admit that in a sense you *do* perceive the penny (or the stick, frock, house, etc.). But, strictly speaking, you don't perceive the penny *directly*. What you *directly* perceive is a sense-datum.

B: That is a purely verbal manoeuvre.

And now it goes on. Once again, don't bother about covering it up; just read it straight through.

B: Unless you can explain to me what you mean by 'direct' and 'indirect perception' you haven't advanced the argument. I could say that, according to the meaning I attach to 'direct perception', I *do* directly perceive the penny. Can you give it another meaning?

A: I don't think that is too difficult. Berkeley made it clear. For example, we say such things as 'I hear a coach', 'I smell onions', 'I taste bacon', but you'll agree that we do not hear, smell or taste things directly. We hear sounds, smell smells, and taste tastes, and through our direct knowledge of sounds, smells and tastes – sense-data – we gain, indirectly, knowledge of such things as coaches, onions and bacon. So now you see why I want to say that we *never* perceive physical things directly; what we directly perceive are sense-data.

B: I can see why you might want to say that *sometimes* we do not perceive physical things directly. But according to Berkeley's sense of 'directly perceive' it is obviously false that we *never* do. Sometimes we hear (not coaches but) the sound they make; sometimes (perhaps) we might see (not a coach but) the reflection it makes, but sometimes we just see coaches. Directly. Or sometimes we bang into them, and then we touch them – directly.

A: No, no. According to the meaning I am giving to 'direct perception' we always directly perceive sense-data, not the physical objects.

B: Then the meaning you are giving the term 'direct perception' is *not* Berkeley's. So you still haven't told me what you mean by it; so we are back with *two* technical terms, 'direct perception' and 'sense-data', neither of which has been explained. [Cf. (ii) on page 112.]

Summary: As if continuing from page 112, A concedes that in a *sense* I perceive physical objects, but maintains that this is merely indirect perception: what I *directly* perceive, he says, are sense-data. B points out that until a meaning has been given to 'direct perception' this is a purely verbal manoeuvre, and certainly will *not*, on its own, show what the term 'sense-data' means, nor that we need it. A sense *can* be given to 'direct and indirect perception' *à la* Berkeley: developing his argument, A could maintain that hearing, smelling, tasting are all cases of ⌐indirectly perceiving¬ the things that cause the sounds, smells and tastes that are ⌐directly perceived¬. A tried to conclude that sense-data, not physical objects, are what we always ⌐directly perceive¬, in this sense, but B points out that, according to this sense of the term 'directly perceive', this is obviously false. Sometimes we hear (not coaches but) the sounds they make, but sometimes we just see and touch coaches. Directly. A then tries to maintain that he means 'direct perception' in some *other* sense, a sense in which it *is* true that we always directly perceive sense-data and never physical objects, and B points out that this other sense has not yet been given, so we are back with *two* technical terms, neither of which has yet been explained.

Once again, this is a dialogue that can continue in many ways. One way in which it can go on involves A giving up the thesis that we never directly perceive physical objects, and involves noticing, with B, that they seem to have produced an argument which suggests a distinction between the five senses: on the one hand there are smell, taste and hearing, which do not involve ⌐direct perception¬ of physical objects, and on the other hand there are sight and touch, which do. We begin to think that perhaps we could communicate pretty well with the Martians as long as they had sight and touch, and that it wouldn't matter much if they didn't have smell, taste and hearing. Remembering that we can communicate with the blind we can be led to distinguish further between sight and touch. Perhaps touch is in some way fundamental to our knowledge of the world around us: for instance it has been suggested that there is at least one physical object whose existence I cannot doubt, and that is (contrary to Descartes) my own body. And I find out about the existence of other physical objects by finding out that I can move *this* one at will, but not others, and that others get in the way of my moving this one.

But, once again, I imagine the dialogue continuing differently. I suppose that my sense-data philosopher A continues to insist that we never ⌐directly perceive¬ physical objects. We can see that he doesn't mean 'directly perceive' in Berkeley's sense. What other sense of the term can he possibly have in mind? This takes us to the next section.

3.5   INTRODUCTION OF SENSE-DATA THROUGH CERTAINTY AND HALLUCINATIONS

Back on page 114 I allowed that a philosopher following Berkeley *would* succeed in giving a sense to the technical terms 'direct' and 'indirect perception', but said that it still wasn't at all clear why he wanted them. Well, perhaps he wants them to draw a distinction between a sort of perception which yields *certainty*, and a sort of perception which, relying on inferences, does not yield certainty, or knowledge, but only belief or opinion. The idea is to define what you ⌐directly perceive¬ as something about which you can be certain; and this contrasts with inferences one may draw from what is ⌐directly perceived¬, which one can't be certain about, because the inference may break down.

Suppose I say, 'I hear the sound of horses' hooves; from this I infer that there are horses somewhere near. So I know there are horses somewhere near.' Or one of the witnesses in court says, 'I heard the accused's typewriter going at 3 p.m.; from that I inferred that he was in his room typing at that time. I know he was in because I heard him.' Now (i) are these inferences that can break down? (ii) Are the claims to knowledge justified?●

PRELIMINARY ANSWER

If you said (i) No and (ii) Yes, imagine that in the first case I am not in the street but in the BBC sound studio, and that in the second case the accused has, not only a typewriter, but a tape recorder. Now what is your answer?●

ANSWER

(i) Yes, these are inferences that can break down. Hence (ii) No, the claims to knowledge are not, or at least not always, justified.

So here is a thought connected with knowledge, or certainty – we can be certain that we heard a sound as of horses' hooves, or a typewriter (and, similarly, that we smelt a smell as of frying onions, or tasted a taste as of bacon) but that does *not* give us certainty as to the presence of horses, or a man typing, or frying onions or bacon (because perhaps the smells and tastes are synthetic).

But at *this* stage in the thought, certainty *is* given by seeing and touching. One doesn't need to be a sceptic to say that moving from a sound to the presence of e.g. horses, is an inference, and one that can break down. At this stage one is not being sceptical, but just sensible, and hence, though we say that we can't be certain while all we have to go on is the sound, we say we can be certain when the horses gallop into full view from around the corner and knock us down. Then we see and touch the horses and we know, we are certain.

So, so far we have an ordinary and sensible notion of 'direct perception' according to which direct perception gives certainty. The list of things we directly perceive is – sounds, smells, tastes, and (for seeing and touching) horses, etc., i.e. physical things.

But remember that the philosopher who is motivated to introduce sense-data is a philosopher who has been affected by the sceptic's arguments concerning hallucinations. So he will *not* think that when we see and touch the horses we *know*, for he will agree with the sceptic that we cannot be absolutely certain that we are seeing or touching a horse. Why not? Because, he will say, it is possible that you are hallucinating. Even when you seem to be seeing and touching a horse you cannot be certain; therefore, you never directly perceive such things as horses, because direct perception, by definition, is that which gives certainty.

Well, we might say in reply, if direct perception has to be what gives you *that* sort of certainty, that is, Cartesian certainty, then we never directly perceive anything. You can't put sounds, smells and tastes on the list, because I can hallucinate a sound, or a smell, or a taste, as easily as I can hallucinate a horse, or a dagger or water in the desert. So I never directly perceive anything.

But the philosopher introducing sense-data has a reply to that. He says, 'But when you are hallucinating, you are seeing *something*, the appearance of a dagger, a mental dagger, and you *can* be certain of that, as you can't about seeing a real physical thing. And if you are in the desert, and hallucinate, not the *sight* of water, but the *sound* of splashing fountains, you are still hearing *something*. Not, I grant you, a real sound, which someone else could hear, and which could be recorded on a tape recorder, but an apparent sound, an imaginary sound, a sound in your head. And you can be absolutely certain about that, as you can't be about hearing a real objective sound. This sort of seeing, this sort of hearing, gives absolute Cartesian certainty, and it is what I mean by direct perception.'

Do you agree with this? Do you agree that when Macbeth has a visual hallucination of a dagger there are *two* things in the situation, Macbeth, and the

117

appearance of a dagger (or an apparent dagger), related in such a way that the first thing, Macbeth, directly perceives the second thing, the apparent dagger? Or do you think that when Macbeth has a visual hallucination there is only one thing in the situation, Macbeth, who believes (falsely) that he is seeing a dagger? If I am in the desert and have an auditory hallucination of splashing fountains, do you think there are two things in the situation, me, and the sound that only I can hear; or just one thing, me, falsely believing that I am hearing a fountain? Just think about this for a moment before reading on.●

If you are tempted to think of the apparent dagger, and the apparent sound as *things*, which are perceived, the sense-data philosopher is about to sweep you behind the veil of perception. For his argument will continue this way: 'Ordinary perception and hallucination have something in common. In both cases there is something about which one can be absolutely certain. When you look at a table you can't be absolutely certain what you are seeing is rectangular. But what you can be absolutely certain about is that you are seeing something that *appears* rectangular; you can be certain you are seeing the appearance a rectangular thing would present viewed from the angle you are supposing yourself to be at. When you look at a shiny tomato you can't be absolutely certain that what you are seeing is a shiny tomato, but what you can be certain about is the look of a shiny tomato. And, in general, when you are looking at a dagger, and Macbeth is hallucinating a dagger, what you both have in common is that there is, for each of you, *something* in the situation about which you can be absolutely certain; each of you is seeing *something* – the appearance of a dagger, or what seems to you to be a dagger.'

Now do you see how that move sweeps us all behind the veil of perception? We had supposed that in ordinary perception there were just two things in the situation, e.g. me, and the table I am looking at, which may appear different, or present a different appearance, as we say, according to the angle from which I look at it. But now it turns out that there are perhaps *three* things. There is me, and the table I'm looking at, AND the appearance it presents. And the-appearance-it-presents, or the apparent table, is *always* the thing I see. I never get to see the table, it is hidden from me by the veil of appearances. I never see the shiny tomato, but only its look. I never, even when they are really there, hear the sound of splashing fountains, but only the imaginary sound in my head, for it is only about *it* that, in common with the man who has an auditory hallucination of splashing fountains, I can be certain. I never feel my own leg, but only my own phantom leg, as the man who still feels something after his leg has been cut off, feels *his* phantom leg. My own leg is, as it were, shrouded in a veil of phantom legs.

How did this mistake come about? Looking back, can you pick on the moves we should have questioned?

It came about when we allowed the sense-data philosopher to talk about appearances and looks and hallucinatory daggers and phantom limbs and imaginary sounds as *things*, in each case the *thing*, the datum, about which one could be absolutely certain, the *thing* one directly perceived. As soon as we admitted them as things we reduplicated everything around us; instead of there being simply me and the table, we allowed me and the table *and* the table's appearance. And as soon as we admitted them as the things we directly perceived, we cut ourselves off from the world around us, and stranded ourselves behind the veil of perception.

Here are some of the moves we should have questioned. We should not have allowed the sense-data philosopher to say that Macbeth saw something. We should have insisted on saying that he didn't see anything, that this is part of what is meant by saying that he *hallucinated* (rather than e.g. misperceived) a dagger. There were not two things in the situation, Macbeth and his hallucinatory dagger, but just one thing, Macbeth, believing, falsely, that he was seeing a dagger.

Should we deny that hallucination and ordinary perception have something in common? Well, I think we could admit that. What they have in common is that they both involve having sensations or sense-experiences. If, crazed with thirst in the desert, I hallucinate the sound of fountains I do have something in common with someone who actually hears splashing fountains, and nothing in common with someone who sees them. What I have in common with the person who actually hears fountains is that we are both having auditory sensations. I have nothing in common with the person who actually sees them (except, perhaps, the belief that there are fountains around) because I am having auditory sensations and he is having visual ones.

Should we deny that what hallucination and ordinary perception have in common is that there is something in the situation which we can each know with absolute certainty? Well, we might deny this because we didn't want to play the sceptic's game about knowledge and absolute certainty. We might want to say: no, that's not what hallucination and ordinary perception have in common. In ordinary perception there is something I can know with absolute certainty, that I am, for example, seeing a tomato; whereas in hallucination there is nothing that can be *known* at all; Macbeth doesn't *know* he sees a dagger, because there's no dagger – he's just wrong.

But suppose we play the sceptic's game, and let ourselves be driven back to the point where (though knowing perfectly well we are seeing a tomato) we say that what we are absolutely certain about is that, in each case, 'It seems to me as if I was seeing a tomato.' Then we could allow that what the man who hallucinates a tomato, and the man who really sees one, have in common is that they can each be absolutely certain about the truth of the sentence 'It seems to me as if I were seeing a tomato.' However, note that in this sentence nothing is said about seeing, i.e. perceiving, anything. We have not committed ourselves to a datum in the situation, a thing which is (directly) perceived, about which we can be absolutely certain. We have only committed ourselves to saying something about how it is with us.

Summary: There might be another sense of direct perception that the sense-data philosopher has in mind. He may think of ⌜direct perception⌝ as that which, by definition, yields certainty. If he is talking about ordinary certainty, then this is perfectly sensible, and, as in the preceding section, yields the conclusion that what we directly perceive are (real) sounds, smells and tastes and (for seeing and touching) physical things. (So once again it would *not* be true that we never directly perceive physical things.) But the sort of certainty he is after is Cartesian certainty. He wants direct perception to yield Cartesian truths. We say, well if that is how you are going to define it, there is no such thing as direct perception. 'I perceive such and such' is never a Cartesian truth, but always open to the sceptic's doubts. But the sense-data philosopher thinks he *has* found an area of Cartesian truths. Even when Macbeth is hallucinating, he says, he is still seeing some *thing*, a datum, of which he can be absolutely certain, which he directly perceives. He can claim, 'I perceive an apparent dagger, the appearance of a dagger' and the sceptic cannot shake him. And the same is true of ordinary perception. Anyone can claim safely to see the appearance of a tomato. These things about which we can be certain, that we directly perceive, are data: sense-data. The list of sense-data then consists of imaginary sounds (not real ones) or apparent ones; imaginary or apparent smells and tastes; appearances and looks of tomatoes and daggers; phantom limbs and so on.

The mistaken move is the introduction of hallucinatory daggers, or the appearances of tomatoes, as *things*. When Macbeth hallucinates he is not seeing something, let alone an apparent dagger. He is not seeing anything; it merely seems to him as if he were seeing a dagger. There is something (as we say) about which he can be absolutely certain, but it is not a *thing*, the apparent dagger. What Macbeth can be absolutely certain about is that it seems to him as if he were seeing a dagger. This is also true of ordinary perception. If I play the sceptic's game I can say that when I see a tomato, all I am absolutely certain of is that it seems to me as if I were seeing a tomato. But that is not a claim to see or perceive anything. So we still have no Cartesian truths of the form 'I perceive a such and such.'

3.6   CONCLUSION

What has the sense-data philosopher now got? Well, he has perhaps found some Cartesian truths. They are of the form 'It seems to me as if I were perceiving a such and such.' But these Cartesian truths have two unsatisfactory aspects.

One unfortunate thing about them is that they do not mention a datum. Part of the point of introducing sense-data was that they were supposed to be *data* – little bits of evidence or information that we pieced together to build up our knowledge of the world around us, whose great virtue was to be that we could be absolutely certain about them. They were to provide the sort of foundation of which Descartes would have approved, and show how we acquired our knowledge, brick by brick, datum by datum. Well, we have perhaps found some Cartesian truths, so we have the certainty advantage, but since the certainty is not certainty about *data*, we cannot use them to show how our knowledge is built upon them.

The other unfortunate thing about them is that, far from looking like truths we *could* start with, in building up knowledge, they seem to presuppose that a whole lot of other truths are already known. How could I know that it seemed to me as if I were seeing a tomato without already knowing what it was like actually to see a tomato? (Compare – how could I know that something seemed to taste of pineapples if I had never tasted a pineapple? How could I know that I seemed to be hearing splashing fountains if I didn't know what fountains were, or what splashing water sounded like?)

The sense-data philosopher got himself into this unsatisfactory position, of finding himself with Cartesian truths that don't do the job he wanted them to do, because, right at the beginning,[1] he *conceded* to the sceptic that the ordinary justification we give for our statements about the external world is not good enough, and set off in pursuit of the false god of a better justification, based on unshakeable foundations. This false god is largely (though not entirely) of Descartes' making, and ever since him, philosophers have found it hard to resist sacrificing common sense on its shrine. In a way, that is not silly, for one thing Descartes taught us was that we must not dogmatically assert that what common sense says is true, or that the ordinary justification of our claims to knowledge never lets us down. The middle road is neither to abandon common sense and ordinary justification entirely, nor to accept them unquestioned, but to subject them to cautious and critical enquiry.

If you would like a glimpse of what such an enquiry would be like, and also something to pull Unit 13 and this one together, try the Whiteley extract in your *Supplementary Texts*. A number of the developmental-testing students reported that they found it very helpful and clear.

If you would like more than a glimpse then you must persist with philosophy and go on to do some of the other courses which contain it.

Epilogue

Here, at the end of the philosophy block, I really want to push two things – a final summary exercise, and your re-reading of the Russell extract for the 'after-effects' – but I know that this has been a long and tough unit, and I also know

---

[1] Page 106.

that some people just do find sense-data very tiresome. If you are suffering *badly* from 'end-of-block' fatigue then I suggest you stick with just re-reading the Russell extract, because this is more likely to cheer you up and convince you that you really have learned something from this unit. Nearly all the developmental-testing students who did re-read it found it *very* rewarding.

I have given you (on page 124) a set of line references in Russell correlated with section numbers and page references to the unit, *not* for you to measure yourself against, but because I thought you might like to use it for looking things up. You might also find re-reading the Russell, with the cross-references, useful for revision. It is *not* supposed to be a complete set.

If you are not completely fatigued, re-read the summaries on pp. 111–12, 116, 119–20 and 122–23 and *then* try the after-effects of the unit on Russell.

And finally, if you are still keeping up, here is the last set of questions leading to a summary. (By all means refer back to the first three summaries mentioned above.)

Final summary questions, covering Part 3 of this unit

1	How did A first try to introduce the term 'sense-data'?	p. 110
2	What did B reply?	p. 110
3	How did A try to argue against B's reply?	p. 111
4	What premise in A's argument did B attack?	p. 111
5	What did A try next?	p. 112
6	B's response?	p. 112
7	Berkeley's argument as developed by A? His attempted conclusion?	p. 115
8	B's reply?	pp. 115–16
9	A new definition of 'directly perceive' connected with certainty?	p. 116
10	According to this definition, what things can we sensibly be said to directly perceive?	p. 117
11	Does the sense-data philosopher, influenced by scepticism, agree that these are the things we directly perceive in his sense?	p. 117
12	Why not?	p. 117
13	What things do we say are directly perceived in his sense? (Do we agree that 'I perceive such and such' can be a Cartesian truth?)	p. 117

(1) A began by introducing the term 'sense-data' to mean 'objects of perception', that is, 'what we perceive'. (2) B replied that we did not need such a term; 'physical objects' is the term that applies to objects of perception, since physical objects are what we perceive. (3) A denied this, and tried to use the argument from illusion to show that, e.g., when I look at a straight stick in water *what I see* is bent, and hence not the straight stick (the physical object) but something else, for which we need the term 'sense-datum'. (4) B attacked the premise that, e.g., what I see is bent. He pointed out that there is no bent stick to be seen; what I see is the straight stick looking bent. (Similarly he denies that what I see is elliptical; what I see is the round penny which may look round, or elliptical, or like a thin brown line.) So in all cases, what I see, perceive, just is the physical object. (5) A concedes that in a *sense* I perceive the physical object, but maintains that this is merely indirect perception; what I directly perceive are sense-data. (6) B points out that until a meaning has been given to 'direct perception', this is a purely verbal manoeuvre. (7) A sense can be given to 'direct and indirect perception' *à la* Berkeley; developing his argument, A could maintain that hearing, smelling and tasting are all cases of ⌜indirectly perceiving⌝ the things that cause the sounds, smells and tastes that are ⌜directly perceived⌝. A tries to conclude that sense-data and *not* physical objects are what we always ⌜directly perceive⌝ in this sense, but (8) B points out that, according to this sense, this is obviously false. Sometimes we hear (not coaches but) the sound they make, but sometimes we just see and touch coaches. Directly. (If A continues to insist that we *never* perceive physical objects directly, he can't mean 'directly perceive' in Berkeley's sense. What other sense of the term can he possibly have in mind?) (9) What he might have in mind is that ⌜direct perception⌝, by definition, yields certainty or knowledge, whereas ⌜indirect perception⌝ doesn't. (10) If he is talking about ordinary certainty, this is perfectly sensible, and, as in the earlier argument ((8) above), yields the conclusion that what we ⌜directly perceive⌝ are (real) sounds, smells and tastes and (for seeing and touching) physical things. (11) The sense-data philosopher, influenced by scepticism, does not agree that we ⌜directly perceive⌝ physical things in his sense of 'directly perceive' because (12) in his sense ⌜direct perception⌝ must yield Cartesian truths: not ordinary certainty, but ⌜absolute⌝ certainty. (13) We say that if that is how he defines it, there is no such thing as direct perception. 'I perceive such and such' is never a Cartesian truth, and hence there isn't anything we 'directly perceive' in his sense. (14) But the sense-data philosopher thinks there are things we directly perceive and that 'I perceive such and such' can be a Cartesian truth. (15) His argument is that even when Macbeth is hallucinating he is still seeing *something*, the appearance of a dagger, or an apparent dagger; this is some thing, a datum, of which he can be absolutely certain. And similarly in ordinary perception: I can always be safe in claiming that I see the appearance of a tomato; its appearance is something of which I can be absolutely certain, some thing I directly perceive. (16) The false move is the introduction of the apparent dagger, or the appearances of tomatoes, as *things*. When Macbeth hallucinates a dagger he is not seeing anything, let alone an apparent dagger. When I retreat to that about which I can be absolutely certain in ordinary perception, I retreat to 'It seems to me as if I were seeing a tomato.' (17) That sort of remark, 'It seems to me as if I were perceiving a tomato/a dagger', is what we are left with. It is, perhaps, a Cartesian truth, but (a) it does not mention a datum which is directly perceived and (b) it does not

seem to be the sort of truth which could serve as the foundation on which to built up a system of knowledge, since it presupposes that other truths are already known. How can I know that it seems to be as *if* I were seeing a tomato without knowing what it is to see a tomato? (18) The bad thing we get from Descartes is the idea that our common-sense beliefs and ordinary justification of our claims to knowledge are no good, and that what we ought to be looking for is better justification based on unshakeable foundations. (19) The good thing we get from Descartes is that we should not let our common-sense beliefs and ordinary justifications pass unquestioned. (20) What we should do is, not abandon them, but subject them to cautious and critical enquiry.

Finally, as another 'after-effect', I should like you to notice how the above summary is almost entirely a summary of *arguments*. If you were able to answer as many as *half* the questions, you have already started to philosophize competently. And that means you have come a long way in three weeks, from when you read, in the introduction to Unit 13, that the only way to philosophize was to jump in at the deep end. You are swimming.

THE RUSSELL EXTRACT

In the left-hand column are line numbers of the extract from Russell's *The Problems of Philosophy* as reprinted in your *Supplementary Texts* (pp. 94–95). In the right-hand column are section and page references to corresponding passages in this unit (and elsewhere).

Lines in Russell	*Sections and pages in Unit 15, etc.*
1–5	Section 1.3, Question 3 (pp. 89–90) and Unit 13, part 2
17–21	Section 3.3, the dialogue (pp. 110–11)
46–49	Unit 13, part 2
59–117	Section 1.5, especially the shine on the tomato (page 94); all of section 2.3, and especially the last but one paragraph ('But of course . . .', page 103)
118–133	Section 2.4, the question and answer on pp. 104–05 ('Now go through . . . a forest of thick trees.')
134–159	Section 2.2. (Also Television Programme 15, on perception)
169–180	Section 3.4
181	Section 3.5, pp. 116–17 (up to '. . . So I never directly perceive anything.')
182–184	Section 3.1, page 108 ('For consider . . . the palm of his hand.') and section 3.5, page 118 ('Now do you see . . . stranded ourselves behind the veil of perception.')
187–191	All of part 3 of Unit 15, especially section 3.2, section 3.3, section 3.5 and the final summary on pp. 122–23, particularly the answers to questions 7, 8, 10, 15 and 16.

UAA—DON'T FORGET *Oswald Hanfling*

Please have Units 2B and 9 handy for this section.

Bertrand Russell once claimed that in philosophy you start by saying something so simple as not to seem worth saying, and you end up with something so paradoxical that no one will believe it. This is certainly a good description of Russell's own work.

I would like you to look again at some extracts from Russell which you have already read. They are taken from the passage in the *Supplementary Texts*.

. . . let us concentrate attention on the table . . .
Although I believe that the table is 'really' of the
same colour all over, the parts that reflect the light
look much brighter than the other parts, and
some parts look white because of reflected light. I
know that, if I move, the parts that reflect the
light will be different, so that the apparent
distribution of colours on the table will change. It
follows that if several people are looking at the
table at the same moment, no two of them will
see exactly the same distribution of colours,
because no two can see it from exactly the same
point of view, and any change in the point of
view makes some change in the way the light is
reflected . . .

. . . It is evident from what we have found, that
there is no colour which pre-eminently appears to
be *the* colour of the table, or even of any one
particular part of the table – it appears to be of
different colours from different points of view,
and there is no reason for regarding some of these
as more really its colour than others . . .

The *shape* of the table is no better. We are all in
the habit of judging as to the 'real' shapes of
things, and we do this so unreflectingly that we
come to think we actually see the real shapes.
But, in fact, as we all have to learn if we try to
draw, a given thing looks different in shape from
every different point of view . . .

Similar difficulties arise when we consider the
sense of touch. It is true that the table always
gives us a sensation of hardness, and we feel that
it resists pressure. But the sensation we obtain
depends upon how hard we press the table and
also upon what part of the body we press with;
thus the various sensations due to various
pressures or various parts of the body cannot be
supposed to reveal *directly* any definite property
of the table . . .[1]

These extracts contain three arguments marked by 'argument-words' (see UAA, page 39). To begin with, please locate these arguments, marking the relevant argument-words (or phrases). Please note that the first argument has *two* such words or phrases; and then there are two arguments with one in each.

---

[1] Bertrand Russell, *The Problems of Philosophy*, 1912 and 1959, Oxford University Press, pp. 2–3.

Did you get them? The first paragraph has 'it follows' and 'because'. Russell's argument here is rather untidy. He starts with some premises; then, using the phrase 'it follows that . . .', states a conclusion; then, with the word 'because', he again gives some premises. It is none too clear how the second set (or statement) of premises is meant to relate to the first.

The second argument-phrase comes in the second paragraph – 'It is evident from what we have found . . .', making it clear that a conclusion is going to be drawn from the foregoing premises. (Here again there is an untidy follow-up with 'it appears . . .' – but there is no further argument-word here.)

Finally, in paragraph four an argument is signalled by the word 'thus', which here means much the same as 'therefore'. Please look again at Russell's text to check my comments on the three arguments.

Imagine now that you are a course tutor and that Russell is one of your students. What critical comments would you put in the margin of his essay? I would certainly object to some of the things he says; and I wonder if you will agree with me. I shall be objecting to two of the three arguments, to one assertion, and to one matter of punctuation.

Here are some clues. (1) One of the arguments has a fault similar to that which I mentioned on page 58 of UAA – 'The author of AA has mentioned . . .' I shall be be making a similar complaint about the concluding part of paragraph two from Russell. (2) About another argument I shall simply say that I can't see how the conclusion follows from the premises. (3) One (at least) of Russell's *assertions* is a case of 'rash generalization' (UAA, page 14). The one I am thinking of occurs in paragraph three and it involves *two* words or phrases – one less obvious than the other. (4) The matter of punctuation that I have in mind may be obvious. But if necessary, refer to UAA, page 18. Please write suitable 'tutor's comments' in the margin.

My own answer is given in two stages. On the next page you will find a reprint of Russell in which I have merely ringed or marked the relevant words and phrases. Please check your answers against this and revise them where appropriate. Then turn to the next page where there is a further reprint with my comments added.

. . . let us concentrate attention on the table . . . Although I believe that the table is *really* of the same colour all over, the parts that reflect the light look much brighter than the other parts, and some parts look white because of reflected light. I know that, if I move, the parts that reflect the light will be different, so that the apparent distribution of colours on the table will change. It follows that if several people are looking at the table at the same moment, no two of them will see exactly the same distribution of colours, because no two can see it from exactly the same point of view, and any change in the point of view makes some change in the way the light is reflected . . .

. . . It is evident from what we have found, that there is no colour which pre-eminently appears to be *the* colour of the table, or even of any one particular part of the table – it appears to be of different colours from different points of view, and there is no reason for regarding some of these as more really its colour than others . . .

The *shape* of the table is no better. We are all in the habit of judging as to the *real* shapes of things, and we do this so unreflectingly that we come to think we actually see the real shapes. But, in fact, as we all have to learn if we try to draw, a given thing looks different in shape from every different point of view . . .

Similar difficulties arise when we consider the sense of touch. It is true that the table always gives us a sensation of hardness, and we feel that it resists pressure. But the sensation we obtain depends upon how hard we press the table and also upon what part of the body we press with; thus the various sensations due to various pressures or various parts of the body cannot be supposed to reveal *directly* any definite property of the table . . .

When you have compared your answers with my markings, read on and compare my comments.

Why scare-quotes? Don't you really mean really?

. . . let us concentrate attention on the table . . . Although I believe that the table is ℴreallyℴ of the same colour all over, the parts that reflect the light look much brighter than the other parts, and some parts look white because of reflected light. I know that, if I move, the parts that reflect the light will be different, so that the apparent distribution of colours on the table will change. It follows that if several people are looking at the table at the same moment, no two of them will see exactly the same distribution of colours, because no two can see it from exactly the same point of view, and any change in the point of view makes some change in the way the light is reflected . . .

. . . It is evident from what we have found, that there is no colour which pre-eminently appears to be *the* colour of the table, or even of any one particular part of the table – it appears to be of different colours from different points of view, and there is no reason for regarding some of these as more really its colour than others . . .

You have argued that *one* kind of reason won't work. How can this show that there is *no* reason?

The *shape* of the table is no better. We are all in the habit of judging as to the ℴrealℴ shapes of things, and we do this so unreflectingly that we come to think we actually see the real shapes. But, in fact, as we all have to learn if we try to draw, a given thing looks different in shape from every different point of view . . .

Is this true in *all* cases and for *all* things? (Try it with some nearby examples.)

Similar difficulties arise when we consider the sense of touch. It is true that the table always gives us a sensation of hardness, and we feel that it resists pressure. But the sensation we obtain depends upon how hard we press the table and also upon what part of the body we press with; thus the various sensations due to various pressures or various parts of the body cannot be supposed to reveal *directly* any definite property of the table . . .

I can't see how this follows from your premises.

"Thus the various sensations due to various pressures on various parts of the body cannot be supposed to reveal directly any definite property of the table."

Notes

1 Scare-quotes are discussed in UAA, page 18, as well as on page 11 of Unit 13 above.

2 I hope you could see why I marked 'a given thing' as well as 'every'. Russell must mean *any and every* 'given thing'. (See my discussion of such phrases in UAA, page 14, and my comments on the extracts that follow there.)

3 Perhaps you are inclined to think that what Russell says *is*, after all, true in all cases – that 'a given thing looks different in shape from every different point of view'. If so, then please do 'try it with some nearby examples' (as I said in my comment in the margin). All right, I will try it myself. Take that enormous tree outside my window. Seen from here, it has a nicely rounded, even shape. But seen from up the road, it is one-sided and angular; it really does 'look different in shape' from that point of view, just as Russell says. By contrast, however, the ruler in my hand does *not* look different in shape if I turn it from this angle to that. (Perhaps you are one of those who will say, 'Ah, but there is more to it than that.' Never mind. The point is that Russell's r.g. needs *argument* – it is not something to be simply asserted as if it must be plain to anyone.)

ACKNOWLEDGEMENTS

I gratefully acknowledge comments on early drafts of these units from members of the Course Team. I am particularly grateful to the developmental-testing students for their many and varied comments and to Euan Henderson of the Institute of Educational Technology at the Open University for his admirably clear and helpful suggestions as to how to cope with their criticisms.

Grateful acknowledgement is made to the following for permission to reproduce illustrated material:

Unit 13 Figure 2: photograph of bust of Newton in Trinity College, Cambridge; excerpt of text from the Turner Collection, Keele University Library. Figure 3: Camera Press Ltd. Figure 4: bust of Socrates in Museo Nazionale, Naples; Mansell Collection. Pages 22, 23 and 39: from Bernard Brown, *Crown and Law: a Bulletin for Schools,* Department of Education (Schools Publications Branch), Wellington, New Zealand, 1969, page 86 (drawing by Graham Percy); reproduced by courtesy of Graham Percy and the Department of Education (Schools Publications), Wellington, New Zealand. Page 25: cover illustration for John Barth, *Lost in the Funhouse,* by Eduardo Paolozzi; reproduced by courtesy of Eduardo Paolozzi and Penguin Books Ltd. Figure 5: engraving from Descartes' *Opera Philosophica,* 1692; Ronan Picture Library. Figure 6: reproduced by kind permission of the *New Statesman*.

Unit 14 Figure 2: *Giovanni Arnolfini and his Wife,* oil on wood, 1434; reproduced by courtesy of the Trustees, The National Gallery, London. Figure 3: National Portrait Gallery, London. Figure 4: Mansell Collection. Page 77: from *The Adventures of Paddy Pork* by John S. Goodall; reproduced by courtesy of Macmillan Administration (Basingstoke) Ltd and Harcourt Brace Jovanovich Inc, New York.

Unit 15 Figure 1 and page 121: Keystone Press Agency. Figure 3: Eastern Daily Press, Norwich. Figure 5: reproduced by courtesy of Librarie Larousse, Paris. Page 93: René Magritte, *Man in Mirror,* oil on canvas, 1937; The Edward James Foundation, Chichester. Figure 7: Mansell Collection. Page 121: Keystone Press Agency.

A101 AN ARTS FOUNDATION COURSE

ARTS AND SOCIETY IN AN AGE OF INDUSTRIALIZATION

THE OPEN UNIVERSITY

An Arts Foundation Course
Units 13,14 and 15

MASKING CARD FOR UNITS 13, 14 AND 15

(a) *A value judgement* is, roughly, a judgement in which a value word is used.

(b) *A value judgement* is a judgement in which the speaker somehow indicates, expresses, conveys, implies, suggests, or gives away what his preferences, likes or dislikes (roughly values), are.

(c) *A subjective judgement* is a judgement which is not strictly in accordance with the facts.

(d) *A subjective judgement* is a judgement a person makes *because* he is biased, prejudiced and/or influenced by personal feelings.

(e) *A subjective judgement* is a judgement in which the speaker says something about himself as a thinking thing, or as a person.

NB In this context 'the speaker' is a quasi-technical term. It means the person who makes the judgement, regardless of whether he says it – that is, speaks – or says it in a book or makes it to himself. 'The judger' is not English; 'the promulgator of the judgement' is ludicrously heavy, so we use 'the speaker'.

I suggest you use this card when, in Unit 14, I ask you to cover up the page and read line by line. The definitions are printed on the card so that you have them beside you while you read the unit and don't have to keep on flipping back to a page on which they are printed. But in case you lose the card, they are reprinted at the end of Unit 14.